# THE Kellogg's® COOKBOOK

## Goes Beyond the Cereal Bowl

® Kellogg Company

**Kellogg Company, Battle Creek, Michigan 49016**

## acknowledgements

Photography:  *JMT, Inc.,* Battle Creek, Michigan

Photograph locations:  *Win Schuler's Restaurant,* Marshall, Michigan (pages 10-11); *National House Inn,* Marshall, Michigan (pages 20-21, 46-47); *Thomas and Versa Vaccaro* residence, Battle Creek, Michigan (pages 64-65); *Cornwell's Turkey House,* Marshall, Michigan (pages 114-115)

Certain props courtesy of *Godfrey Jewelers,* Battle Creek, Michigan and *Sarkozy Bakery,* Kalamazoo, Michigan

Printed in the United States of America
first edition/first printing
0998-8-2539

**front cover**

tossed salad deluxe, page 67
cranberry sparkler punch, page 13
crunchy party snack, pages 15, 198
save-a-day rolls, page 62
Cornish beef pasties, page 103
Eggo frozen waffles with
    fresh strawberry sauce, page 43

**back cover**

sweet chocolate cake, page 148
double coated chicken, page 119
cinnamon balls, page 171
cherry winks, page 166
ambrosia pie, page 152
date-filled tea ring, page 57
anadama bread, page 52
good and spicy meatballs, page 87

# CONTENTS

# GENERAL
# INFORMATION

# GENERAL INFORMATION

## cooking with Kellogg's – an enduring tradition

Soon after Kellogg's Corn Flakes cereal first appeared on America's breakfast tables, another use for ready-to-eat cereals became apparent. Recognizing that these new breakfast foods could "go beyond the cereal bowl," the Company established a home economics department in 1923. A home economist-dietitian was hired, a small test kitchen was built and soon recipes regularly appeared on the cereal packages and in recipe booklets. Since the original recipe testing facility began functioning, we have outgrown three kitchens. The current Test Center, with its adjacent taste testing room, is equipped with the most modern cooking conveniences.

The popularity of recipes created in these kitchens throughout the years is the reason for "The Kellogg's Cookbook," the most comprehensive collection of Kellogg family-size recipes ever assembled. Each of the 270 recipes and variations selected for these pages was tested and approved in the Kellogg's Home Economics Test Center. You'll find party snacks and beverages, hearty family casseroles, easy-to-make breads, spectacular desserts, a delightful array of cookies and much, much more. A microwave cookery section is also included, with age-old favorites like Molasses Brown Bread and Marshmallow Treats adapted for the contemporary microwave oven.

## our other convenience foods

Aside from recipes using ready-to-eat cereals, we've included a wide selection of recipes made with other great-tasting convenience foods marketed by Kellogg Company. Ready-to-use Corn Flake Crumbs and versatile Croutettes herb seasoned croutons, a popular stuffing for the holiday turkey, are featured in dozens of recipes throughout this cookbook. Eggo brand Frozen Waffles lend themselves deliciously to the "dressed-up" breakfast ideas that are found in the Quick Breads section.

Junket Danish dessert, a fruit-flavored Danish-style pudding and pie filling mix, is a key to the success of luscious desserts such as Fresh Strawberry Pie and delicate Strawberry Danish Tarts. And to complete the recipe selection, we've provided some hot and cold punch recipes, delightfully "spiked" with Salada Teas.

## more than just "good looks"

The fresh crisp crunch of ready-to-eat cereals is an added benefit in many recipes. These grain-based products also contribute a wholesome flavor and an attractive golden brown color when used in cooking.

And because ready-to-eat cereals are a good source of vitamins and minerals, they increase the total nutritional value of recipes. Virtually all Kellogg cereals are fortified with 10% to 25% of the U.S. Recommended Daily Allowances for many essential vitamins and minerals. Kellogg's bran cereals are also rich in dietary fiber.

For many years, Kellogg package labels have included important nutrition information about the product inside. To receive additional information in the form of nutritive values charts, you can write to the Consumer Service Department at Kellogg Company.

## but before you begin . . .

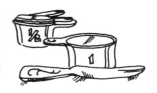

Ready-to-eat cereals are measured using individual graduated measuring cups (those commonly used for dry ingredients). Pour the cereal into the cup and level with the straight edge of a spatula or knife, being careful not to crush the cereal.

You'll note that some recipes call for a short standing period for cereal and liquid mixtures. This important step allows the cereal to be more evenly dispersed throughout the final product. In breads, this helps to produce the desirable fine, even texture.

When a recipe tells you to crush a Kellogg product, there are three easy methods that can be used. First, you can place a measured amount of cereal in a plastic bag or on a sheet of waxed paper and crush with a rolling pin. Second, you can measure the cereal into a glass measuring cup and then crush with a spoon to the measurement called for in the recipe. Or third, if you have an electric blender you can blend the cereal, using a medium setting, for a few seconds or until the specified measurement is achieved.

Don't despair if your recipe calls for 3 cups of a certain cereal when all that's left after breakfast are 2 cups! Just add 1 cup of another cereal having similar physical characteristics. Although slight flavor and texture differences will result, you can expect good results when making substitutions such as Bran Buds cereal for All-Bran cereal, or Product 19 supplement cereal for Corn Flakes cereal. If you're unexpectedly out of Corn Flake Crumbs, try using Corn Flakes cereal, crushed into fine crumbs. It takes about 2 cups of Corn Flakes cereal to make 1/2 cup of crumbs. Many recipes in this cookbook suggest cereal alternatives as a variation of the basic recipe.

## cereal cookery — on your own

The versatility of ready-to-eat cereals in cooking is easy to discover. Use cereals for crispy toppings, crunchy coatings or economical extenders to make many recipes more tasty and nutritious. The following general directions can be used when incorporating cereals into your own favorite recipes.

### crisp toppings

To add a crisp and tasty accent to vegetable or main dish casseroles, combine 1/2 cup crushed ready-to-eat cereal with 2 tablespoons margarine and complementary herbs and spices. Then sprinkle the mixture over your favorite casserole, bake and enjoy!

## crunchy coatings

For a crunchy golden coating on *baked chicken, pork chops* or *fish fillets,* use a ready-to-eat cereal, crushed into coarse or fine crumbs. Add salt, pepper or other seasonings. Dip the chicken pieces, chops or fish into an egg-milk mixture, melted margarine or evaporated milk. Then coat with the crushed cereal and bake. For a crisp and delicious variation when making *biscuits* or *dinner rolls,* just brush the dough with melted margarine and sprinkle with a crushed ready-to-eat cereal before baking. The cereal can be mixed with herbs, spices or shredded cheese for even more flavor. *Drop cookies* can also be varied by coating spoonfuls of dough with crushed cereal before baking.

## economical extenders

To make a main dish go just a little further, simply add 1/4 to 1/2 cup of crushed ready-to-eat cereal to a pound of ground meat or flaked fish when making loaves, patties or croquettes.

## delicious crusts

Most ready-to-eat cereals make a delicious crust for refrigerated or frozen desserts. In a small saucepan, cook 1/3 cup margarine or butter and 1/4 cup sugar until the mixture boils, stirring constantly. Add 1/8 to 1/4 tea-spoon ground cinnamon and orange or lemon peel, if desired. Combine with 1 cup of finely crushed ready-to-eat cereal and press the mixture firmly into a 9 x 9 x 2-inch square pan or pie pan. Chill thoroughly before filling with pudding, slightly softened ice cream or frozen yogurt. Chill or freeze until serving time and garnish with fresh or canned fruit, if desired.

**It's time now to venture "beyond the cereal bowl" . . .**

# APPETIZERS & BEVERAGES

# APPETIZERS & BEVERAGES

Is there a better way to whet your appetite than with a taste-tempting appetizer and a refreshing beverage? Served alone or before a meal, an array of hot and cold appetizers and beverages can complement each other as well as the repast that will follow.

1. cheese 'n mushroom waffle wedges, p. 18
2. gazpacho soup, p. 16
3. crunchy bran jumble, p. 15
4. lemon tea delight, p. 14
5. Indian cheese ball, p. 18

# apricot swizzle

> 3 tablespoons Salada Instant 100% Tea
> 1/4 cup sugar
> 1 can (12 oz.) apricot nectar
> 2 cups cold water
> 1 can (6 oz.) frozen lemonade concentrate, thawed
> 2 cups ginger ale, chilled

● Measure all ingredients except ginger ale into large pitcher. Stir until Instant Tea is dissolved. Chill. Just before serving, gently stir in ginger ale.

Yield:   8 servings, 3/4 cup each

# cranberry sparkler punch

> 6 cups water
> 6 tablespoons Salada Instant 100% Tea
> 1 cup sugar
> 1 cup orange juice
> 4 cups cranberry juice cocktail
> 1/2 teaspoon ground cinnamon
> 1/2 teaspoon ground nutmeg
> 1 bottle (32 oz.) lemon-lime carbonated beverage, chilled
> 2 oranges, sliced
> Ice ring

● Measure water and Instant Tea into large pitcher or gallon container. Stir until Tea is dissolved. Add sugar, orange juice, cranberry juice cocktail, cinnamon and nutmeg. Stir. Chill thoroughly. Just before serving, pour Tea mixture into punch bowl. Gently stir in carbonated beverage. Add sliced oranges and ice ring.

Yield:   32 servings, 1/2 cup each

# lemon tea delight

1 pint lemon sherbet, slightly softened
1/3 cup Salada Instant 100% Tea
2 tablespoons sugar
3 cups cold milk
Lemon slices

● In medium-size mixing bowl or blender, beat sherbet, Instant Tea and sugar until smooth. Add milk, mixing until foamy. Garnish with lemon slices. Serve immediately.

Yield:   5 servings, 1 cup each

# spicy hot tea punch

6-1/2 cups water
1/3 cup lemon juice
2/3 cup orange juice
1 cup sugar
2 teaspoons whole cloves
1 stick cinnamon
1 teaspoon whole allspice
2 Salada Tea Bags

● Combine all ingredients except Tea Bags in large saucepan. Bring to boil. Reduce heat to low and simmer 5 minutes. Add Tea Bags. Steep 5 minutes. Remove Tea Bags and spices. Serve hot.

Yield:   10 servings, 3/4 cup each

# crunchy party snack

      1/2 cup regular margarine or butter

        2 tablespoons Worcestershire sauce

        4 cups Croutettes herb seasoned croutons

        1 cup salted cocktail peanuts

        1 cup thin pretzel sticks

- Melt margarine in large saucepan. Remove from heat. Stir in Worcestershire sauce. Add Croutettes croutons, peanuts and pretzels, tossing gently until well coated.

- Spread mixture evenly in 15-1/2 x 10-1/2 x 1-inch baking pan. Bake in oven at 300° F. about 15 minutes or until crisped and lightly browned. Stir occasionally. Cool completely. Store in tightly covered container.

Yield:  5-1/2 cups

See page 198 for microwave directions.

# crunchy bran jumble

        3 cups Cracklin' Bran cereal

        1 cup salted cocktail peanuts

        1 cup thin pretzel sticks

      1/3 cup regular margarine or butter, melted

        1 tablespoon sesame seed

      1/2 teaspoon ground oregano

        1 teaspoon onion salt

        2 teaspoons Worcestershire sauce

- Measure Cracklin' Bran cereal, peanuts and pretzels into 13 x 9 x 2-inch baking pan. Stir together remaining ingredients. Pour over cereal mixture, stirring until well coated. Bake in oven at 350° F. about 15 minutes. Do not stir. Cool completely. Store in tightly covered container.

Yield:  5 cups

See page 200 for microwave directions.

# gazpacho soup

2 cans (10-3/4 oz. each) condensed tomato soup
2 cups water
1/8 teaspoon rosemary leaves
1/8 teaspoon oregano leaves
1/8 teaspoon basil leaves
1 clove garlic, finely chopped
1/4 cup finely chopped onion
1/4 cup vinegar

*      *      *      *      *

1/4 cup regular margarine or butter
1 clove garlic, split
2 cups Croutettes herb seasoned croutons

*      *      *      *      *

1 medium-size tomato, peeled, coarsely chopped
1 medium-size green pepper, coarsely chopped
1 medium-size cucumber, coarsely chopped
1 hard-cooked egg, coarsely chopped

- Measure first 8 ingredients into large mixing bowl. Stir to combine. Chill.

- While soup is chilling, melt margarine in large frypan over low heat. Add split garlic and Croutettes croutons, stirring until well coated. Cook, stirring frequently, until croutons are crisped and lightly browned. Remove and discard garlic. Set croutons aside to cool.

- Portion tomato, green pepper, cucumber and egg into chilled soup bowls. Pour about 3/4 cup soup over each portion. Top with croutons.

Yield:  8 to 10 servings

16

**VARIATION:**

Fresh Tomato Gazpacho:

>     5 cups peeled, fully ripe, chopped tomatoes
>     1 clove garlic, finely chopped
>   1/4 cup chopped onion
>   1/4 cup vinegar
>     1 can (6 oz.) tomato paste
>     1 teaspoon salt

● Measure 2 cups of the tomatoes and remaining ingredients into blender container. Blend until smooth. Pour into medium-size mixing bowl. Blend remaining tomatoes until smooth. Stir into tomato-onion mixture. Chill thoroughly. Continue as directed in step 2 on page 16.

Yield:   6 to 8 servings


# cherry-plum soup

>     1 can (16 oz.) plums, pitted
>     1 can (16 oz.) dark, sweet, pitted cherries
>       Water
>     1 package (4-3/4 oz.) Junket Danish Dessert, cherry-plum flavor
>     1 stick cinnamon
>   1/2 cup golden seedless raisins

● Drain plums and cherries and save syrup. Set fruits aside.

● Add enough water to syrup to measure 3-1/2 cups. Pour into medium-size saucepan. Stir in contents of Danish Dessert package. Add stick cinnamon. Bring to a full boil over medium heat. Boil 1 minute, stirring constantly. Remove from heat.

● Add drained fruits and raisins. Return to low heat and cook until thoroughly heated. Remove stick cinnamon. Serve hot with whipped topping, if desired.

Yield:   6 servings, 1 cup each

NOTE:   Soup may also be served cold but will be slightly thicker.

# cheese 'n mushroom waffle wedges

1-1/2 cups shredded American cheese
1 jar (2-1/2 oz.) sliced mushrooms, drained
1/4 cup mayonnaise
1 tablespoon finely chopped onion
1/2 teaspoon salt
1/8 teaspoon cayenne pepper
2 teaspoons Worcestershire sauce
1/2 teaspoon prepared mustard
6 Eggo Frozen Waffles

- Stir together all ingredients except Waffles. Spread mixture on Waffles to within 1/4 inch of edge. Place on rack on baking sheet.

- Broil 4 inches from source of heat about 3 minutes or until cheese is melted and Waffles are thoroughly heated. Cut each into 8 pieces. Serve immediately.

Yield: 4 dozen

# Indian cheese ball

1 package (8 oz.) cream cheese, softened
1/2 cup ricotta cheese or dry curd cottage cheese
2 tablespoons chopped chutney or dried apricots
1 tablespoon finely chopped onion
1 teaspoon lemon juice
1/2 teaspoon salt
1/2 teaspoon curry powder
1/2 cup All-Bran cereal or Bran Buds cereal

- In large mixing bowl, beat cream cheese and ricotta cheese until smooth. Stir in chutney, onion, lemon juice, salt and curry powder. Chill until stiff. Shape into ball. Roll ball in All-Bran cereal. Chill. Serve with crackers.

# cheese wafers

3/4 cup regular all-purpose flour
1/2 teaspoon salt
   Dash cayenne pepper
1/2 cup regular margarine or butter, softened
   2 cups (8 oz.) shredded sharp cheddar cheese
1-1/2 cups Rice Krispies cereal

- Stir together flour, salt and pepper. Set aside.

- In large mixing bowl, beat margarine and cheese until very light and fluffy. Stir in Rice Krispies cereal. Add flour mixture, mixing until well combined. Drop by rounded measuring-teaspoon onto ungreased baking sheets. Flatten with fork dipped in flour.

- Bake in oven at 350° F. about 12 minutes or until lightly browned around edges. Remove immediately from baking sheets. Cool on wire racks.

Yield:   about 5 dozen

**VARIATION:**

1-1/2 cups All-Bran cereal may be substituted for the Rice Krispies cereal.

# QUICK BREADS

# QUICK BREADS

Whether for breakfast or brunch, lunch or dinner, appetizer or dessert, quick breads of all kinds have achieved a lasting popularity. Quick-to-mix muffins, loaves and coffee cakes can add sparkle and versatility to your favorite menu.

1. pumpkin nut bread, p. 39
2. frypan bacon bread, p. 31
3. bran muffins, p. 36
4. Eggo frozen waffles with fresh strawberry sauce, p. 43
5. bran cherry nut bread, p. 38
6. surprise muffins, p. 35
7. pecan tea muffins, p. 28
8. molasses brown bread, p. 44
9. marmalade coffee cake, p. 40
10. cherry fritters with cherry sauce, p. 24

# bran banana bread

        **2 cups regular all-purpose flour**
        **1 teaspoon baking powder**
      **1/2 teaspoon baking soda**
      **1/2 teaspoon salt**
  **1-1/2 cups mashed, fully ripe bananas**
  **1-1/2 cups All-Bran cereal or Bran Buds cereal**
     **1/2 cup regular margarine or butter, softened**
     **3/4 cup sugar**
       **2 eggs**
     **1/2 cup coarsely chopped nuts**

- Stir together flour, baking powder, soda and salt. Set aside.

- In small mixing bowl, stir together mashed bananas and All-Bran cereal. Let stand 2 to 3 minutes or until cereal is softened.

- In large mixing bowl, beat margarine and sugar until well blended. Add eggs. Beat well. Mix in cereal mixture. Stir in flour mixture. Stir in nuts. Spread batter evenly in greased 9 x 5 x 3-inch loaf pan.

- Bake in oven at 350° F. about 1 hour or until wooden pick inserted near center comes out clean. Let cool 10 minutes before removing from pan. Cool completely on wire rack before slicing.

Yield:  1 loaf

**VARIATIONS:**

**Bran Flakes Banana Bread:** Substitute 2-1/2 cups 40% Bran Flakes cereal for the 1-1/2 cups All-Bran cereal. Combine 40% Bran Flakes cereal with the mashed bananas in medium-size mixing bowl. Continue as directed above.

**Banana Honey Bread:**  Substitute 2/3 cup honey for the 3/4 cup sugar.

23

# cherry fritters with cherry sauce

    1 can (16 oz.) red, sour, pitted cherries, drained, reserving liquid
1-1/2 cups regular all-purpose flour
    2 teaspoons baking powder
    1 teaspoon salt
  3/4 cup sugar
    1 egg
  3/4 cup milk
    2 teaspoons vegetable oil
  1/2 cup All-Bran cereal or Bran Buds cereal
       Vegetable oil or shortening (for frying)
    1 tablespoon cornstarch
       Water


- Reserve 1/4 cup cherries for sauce. Chop remaining cherries. Set aside.

- Stir together flour, baking powder, salt and 1/4 cup of the sugar. Set aside.

- In large mixing bowl, beat egg slightly. Stir in milk, oil and All-Bran cereal. Let stand 1 to 2 minutes or until cereal is softened. Add flour mixture, stirring until smooth. Stir in chopped cherries.

- Drop by rounded measuring-tablespoon into hot deep oil (375° F.). Fry until golden brown, about 2-1/2 minutes. Drain on absorbent paper.

- For *Cherry Sauce,* combine the remaining 1/2 cup sugar and the cornstarch in small saucepan. Add water to reserved cherry liquid to measure 1 cup liquid. Gradually stir into sugar mixture. Bring to boil. Cook until thickened and clear, stirring constantly. Stir in reserved cherries. Serve with warm fritters.

Yield:  about 24 fritters

NOTE: To reheat fritters, place on baking sheet and bake in oven at 200° F. for 10 to 15 minutes.

# cinnamon crunch coffee cake

   1 cup Corn Flakes cereal

   3 tablespoons regular margarine or butter, melted

   3 tablespoons firmly packed brown sugar

1/2 teaspoon ground cinnamon

      \*     \*     \*     \*     \*

1-1/4 cups regular all-purpose flour

1-1/2 teaspoons baking powder

   1/2 teaspoon salt

     2 teaspoons ground cinnamon

     1 cup Corn Flakes cereal

   1/2 cup shortening

   1/3 cup firmly packed brown sugar

     1 egg

   3/4 cup milk

     1 teaspoon grated orange peel (optional)

- Crush 1 cup Corn Flakes cereal to measure 1/2 cup. Combine crushed cereal, melted margarine, the 3 tablespoons sugar and the 1/2 teaspoon cinnamon. Set aside for topping.

- Stir together flour, baking powder, salt and the 2 teaspoons cinnamon. Set aside.

- Crush the remaining 1 cup cereal to measure 1/2 cup. Set aside.

- In large mixing bowl, beat shortening and the 1/3 cup sugar until light and fluffy. Add egg. Beat well. Mix in the 1/2 cup crushed cereal, the milk and orange peel. Add flour mixture, stirring only until combined. Spread batter evenly in greased 8 x 8 x 2-inch baking pan. Sprinkle with cereal topping, pressing gently into batter.

- Bake in oven at 375° F. about 25 minutes or until wooden pick inserted near center comes out clean. Cool about 5 minutes. Cut into squares. Serve warm.

Yield:   9 servings

**VARIATIONS:**

Stir in 1/2 cup seedless raisins, finely cut dried apricots or finely cut prunes before adding the flour mixture.

# peanut butter bread

**1-1/2 cups regular all-purpose flour**

**3 teaspoons baking powder**

**1/2 teaspoon salt**

**2 cups Raisin Bran cereal**

**1-1/3 cups milk**

**1/3 cup peanut butter**

**1/2 cup sugar**

**1 egg**

**1/4 cup chopped peanuts**

- Stir together flour, baking powder and salt. Set aside.

- Combine Raisin Bran cereal and milk in small mixing bowl. Let stand 1 to 2 minutes or until cereal is softened.

- In large mixing bowl, beat peanut butter and sugar until well blended. Add egg. Beat well. Mix in cereal mixture. Stir in flour mixture. Stir in peanuts. Spread batter evenly in greased 9 x 5 x 3-inch loaf pan.

- Bake in oven at 350° F. about 1 hour or until wooden pick inserted near center comes out clean. Remove from pan. Cool completely on wire rack before slicing.

Yield:   1 loaf

# bran bread with raisins

**1-1/2 cups regular all-purpose flour**

**1 teaspoon baking powder**

**1 teaspoon baking soda**

**1 teaspoon salt**

**1/2 cup sugar**

**1-1/2 cups All-Bran cereal or Bran Buds cereal**

**1-1/2 cups seedless raisins**

**1/4 cup shortening**

**1-1/2 cups very hot water**

**1 egg**

**1 teaspoon vanilla flavoring**

**3/4 cup chopped nuts**

**26**

- Stir together flour, baking powder, soda, salt and sugar. Set aside.

- Measure All-Bran cereal, raisins and shortening into large mixing bowl. Add water, stirring until shortening is melted. Add egg, vanilla and nuts. Beat well. Add flour mixture, stirring only until combined. Spread batter evenly in well-greased 9 x 5 x 3-inch loaf pan.

- Bake in oven at 350° F. about 55 minutes or until wooden pick inserted near center comes out clean. Remove from pan. Cool completely on wire rack before slicing. Or wrap tightly and store overnight before serving.

Yield:   1 loaf

# double apple bread

---

2 cups Apple Jacks cereal

1-1/2 cups regular all-purpose flour

2 teaspoons baking powder

1/2 teaspoon baking soda

1/4 teaspoon salt

1 teaspoon ground cinnamon

1/4 teaspoon ground allspice

1/3 cup regular margarine or butter, softened

1/2 cup sugar

2 eggs

1/2 teaspoon vanilla flavoring

1/2 cup milk

1 cup finely chopped, pared tart apples

- Crush the 2 cups Apple Jacks cereal to measure 1 cup. Place in medium-size mixing bowl. Stir in flour, baking powder, soda, salt, cinnamon and allspice. Set aside.

- In large mixing bowl, beat margarine and sugar until well blended. Add eggs and vanilla. Beat well. Add flour mixture alternately with milk, mixing well after each addition. Fold in apples. Spread batter evenly in greased 9 x 5 x 3-inch loaf pan.

- Bake in oven at 350° F. about 40 minutes or until wooden pick inserted near center comes out clean. Cool 10 minutes before removing from pan. Cool completely on wire rack before slicing.

Yield:   1 loaf

# pecan tea muffins

1 cup regular all-purpose flour
2-1/2 teaspoons baking powder
1/2 teaspoon salt
1/2 teaspoon ground nutmeg
1/4 cup sugar
1 cup All-Bran cereal or Bran Buds cereal
3/4 cup milk
1 egg
1/4 cup shortening
3/4 cup finely chopped pecans

*     *     *     *     *

1 teaspoon ground cinnamon
1/3 cup sugar
1/4 cup regular margarine or butter, melted

- Stir together flour, baking powder, salt, nutmeg and the 1/4 cup sugar. Set aside.

- Measure All-Bran cereal and milk into large mixing bowl. Stir to combine. Let stand 1 to 2 minutes or until cereal is softened. Add egg and shortening. Beat well. Stir in pecans.

- Add flour mixture, stirring only until combined. Portion batter evenly into 24 greased 1-1/2-inch muffin-pan cups.

- Bake in oven at 400° F. about 15 minutes or until lightly browned. Remove from pans.

- Stir together cinnamon and the 1/3 cup sugar. Quickly dip tops of hot muffins in melted margarine. Then dip in cinnamon-sugar mixture. Serve warm.

Yield:   24 muffins

**VARIATION:**

Muffins may also be prepared using 2-1/2-inch muffin-pan cups. Bake at 400° F. about 25 minutes. Yield:  12 muffins

# corn crumb muffins

1-1/3 cups Corn Flake Crumbs
1-1/3 cups regular all-purpose flour
    4 teaspoons baking powder
  3/4 teaspoon salt
  1/3 cup sugar
    1 egg
1-1/2 cups milk
  1/3 cup vegetable oil

- Stir together Corn Flake Crumbs, flour, baking powder, salt and sugar. Set aside.

- In large mixing bowl, beat egg slightly. Stir in milk and oil. Add Crumbs mixture. Mix well. Let stand about 2 minutes. Portion batter evenly into 12 greased 2-1/2-inch muffin-pan cups.

- Bake in oven at 400° F. about 25 minutes or until golden brown. Serve warm.

Yield:   12 muffins

## VARIATIONS:

**Fruit Crumb Muffins:**   Add 1/2 cup seedless raisins, finely cut dates or other dried fruit to egg mixture before adding dry ingredients.

**Cheese Crumb Muffins:**   Add 1/2 cup shredded American cheese to egg mixture before adding dry ingredients.

**Nutty Crumb Muffins:**  Add 1/2 cup chopped nuts to dry ingredients before adding to egg mixture.

**Hawaiian Crumb Muffins:**   Add 1/4 cup flaked coconut, 1/4 cup chopped nuts and 1 teaspoon ground ginger to dry ingredients before adding to egg mixture.

**Sweet Top Muffins:**   Mix together 1/4 teaspoon ground cinnamon and 2 tablespoons sugar. Sprinkle 1/2 teaspoon cinnamon-sugar mixture over top of each muffin before baking.

**Marmalade Crumb Muffins:**   Press 1 rounded teaspoon orange marmalade or other jam into top of each muffin before baking.

**Blueberry Muffins:**   Fold 1 cup fresh or frozen blueberries into batter.

# lemon nut tea cake

**1-1/2 cups Corn Flakes cereal**
**1-1/2 cups regular all-purpose flour**
**1 teaspoon baking powder**
**1/2 teaspoon salt**
**1/2 cup regular margarine or butter, softened**
**1-1/4 cups sugar**
**2 eggs**
**1/2 cup milk**
**Grated peel of 1 lemon**
**1/2 cup finely chopped walnuts**

- Crush the 1-1/2 cups Corn Flakes cereal to measure 1/2 cup. Set aside.
- Stir together flour, baking powder and salt. Set aside.
- In large mixing bowl, beat margarine and sugar until light and fluffy. Add eggs. Beat well. Stir in milk. Add flour mixture, mixing until combined. Stir in grated lemon peel, walnuts and crushed cereal. Pour into greased 8 x 8 x 2-inch baking pan.
- Bake in oven at 325° F. about 40 minutes or until wooden pick inserted near center comes out clean. Serve with *Tangy Lemon Sauce.*

Yield:   12 servings

# tangy lemon sauce

**1/2 cup sugar**
**1 tablespoon cornstarch**
**1 cup water**
**3 tablespoons regular margarine or butter**
**1 teaspoon grated lemon peel**
**3 tablespoons lemon juice**

30

- In small saucepan, combine sugar, cornstarch and water. Cook over medium heat, stirring constantly, until thickened and clear. Remove from heat. Add margarine, lemon peel and lemon juice, stirring until margarine melts. Serve warm or cooled.

Yield: 1-1/3 cups

# frypan bacon bread

**1 cup Corn Flake Crumbs**
**1-1/2 cups regular all-purpose flour**
**3 teaspoons baking powder**
**1 teaspoon salt**
**3 tablespoons sugar**
**3/4 lb. bacon, diced**
**Vegetable oil**
**2 eggs, slightly beaten**
**1 cup milk**

- In large mixing bowl, stir together Corn Flake Crumbs, flour, baking powder, salt and sugar. Set aside.

- Fry bacon in 8-1/2-inch frypan (with oven-safe handle) until crisp. Place bacon on absorbent paper. Reserve drippings.

- Add oil to bacon drippings to measure 1/2 cup. Pour into small bowl. Stir in eggs and milk. Add to Crumbs mixture, stirring only until combined. Fold in half the bacon bits.

- Spread evenly in the frypan in which the bacon was cooked. Sprinkle top with remaining bacon bits.

- Bake in oven at 400° F. about 30 minutes or until golden brown and wooden pick inserted near center comes out clean. While still warm, loosen edges and cut into 12 wedges. Serve immediately.

Yield: 12 servings

**VARIATION:**

*Frypan Bacon Bread* may be baked in greased 9 x 9 x 2-inch baking pan. Cut into squares to serve.

# master breads mix

4 cups regular all-purpose flour

3 tablespoons baking powder

1-1/2 teaspoons salt

1 cup sugar

3-1/4 cups All-Bran cereal or Bran Buds cereal

In large container, stir all ingredients together. Store tightly covered. Use in *Coffee Cake, Muffins* or *Pancakes* (recipes follow).

Yield:  6 cups *Master Breads Mix*

# coffee cake

1/2 cup firmly packed brown sugar

2 tablespoons regular all-purpose flour

2 teaspoons ground cinnamon

1/4 cup chopped nuts

1/4 cup flaked coconut

2 tablespoons regular margarine or butter, melted

\*          \*          \*          \*          \*

1 egg

1/4 cup vegetable oil

1-1/4 cups milk

2 cups Master Breads Mix (see above)

- Measure brown sugar, flour, cinnamon, nuts and coconut into small mixing bowl. Stir to combine. Add margarine. Mix well. Set aside for topping.

- In large mixing bowl, beat egg slightly. Add oil and milk. Beat well. Add *Master Breads Mix.* Mix thoroughly. Let stand 1 to 2 minutes or until cereal is softened. Spread batter evenly in greased 9 x 9 x 2-inch baking pan. Sprinkle brown sugar mixture over batter.

- Bake in oven at 350° F. about 45 minutes or until wooden pick inserted near center comes out clean. Cool about 5 minutes. Cut into squares. Serve warm.

Yield:  8 servings

# muffins

**1 egg**
**1/4 cup vegetable oil**
**1 cup milk**
**2 cups Master Breads Mix (see page 32)**

- In large mixing bowl, beat egg slightly. Add oil and milk. Beat well. Add *Master Breads Mix,* stirring only until combined. Let stand 1 to 2 minutes or until cereal is softened. Portion batter evenly into 12 greased 2-1/2-inch muffin-pan cups.

- Bake in oven at 400° F. about 25 minutes or until lightly browned.

Yield:   12 muffins


# pancakes

**1 egg**
**1/4 cup vegetable oil**
**1-3/4 cups milk**
**2 cups Master Breads Mix (see page 32)**

- In large mixing bowl, beat egg until foamy. Add oil and milk. Beat well. Add *Master Breads Mix.* Mix thoroughly. Let stand 1 to 2 minutes or until cereal is softened.

- Dip up batter, using 1/4 cup for each pancake. Cook on greased and preheated griddle, turning once, until golden brown on both sides. Serve immediately.

Yield:   14 pancakes

# cinnamon topped prune muffins

1-1/4 cups regular all-purpose flour

1/3 cup sugar

3-1/2 teaspoons baking powder

1 teaspoon salt

2 cups Product 19 multivitamin and iron supplement cereal

1-1/4 cups milk

1 egg

1/3 cup shortening

3/4 cup cut, pitted prunes

1/8 teaspoon ground cinnamon

1 tablespoon sugar

● Stir together flour, the 1/3 cup sugar, the baking powder and salt. Set aside.

● Crush the 2 cups Product 19 supplement cereal to measure 1 cup. Place in large mixing bowl. Stir in milk. Let stand 2 to 3 minutes or until supplement cereal is softened. Add egg and shortening. Beat well. Stir in prunes. Add flour mixture, stirring only until combined. Portion batter evenly into 12 greased 2-1/2-inch muffin-pan cups. Stir together cinnamon and the 1 tablespoon sugar. Sprinkle over muffin batter.

● Bake in oven at 400° F. about 20 minutes or until golden brown. Serve warm.

Yield: 12 muffins

**VARIATION:**

For plain muffins, omit prunes and cinnamon-sugar topping.

# easy four-grain pancakes

2 eggs

2 cups milk

2 tablespoons vegetable oil

4 cups Product 19 multivitamin and iron supplement cereal

1 cup dry pancake mix

- In small mixing bowl, beat eggs until foamy. Stir in milk and oil. Set aside.

- Crush the 4 cups Product 19 supplement cereal to measure 1 cup. Place in medium-size mixing bowl. Stir in pancake mix. Add milk mixture, stirring until batter is almost smooth.

- Dip up batter, using 1/4 cup for each pancake. Cook on greased and preheated griddle, turning once, until golden brown on both sides. Serve with warm pancake syrup.

Yield:  12 pancakes

**VARIATION:**

**Pancake Stacks:**  For each serving, layer 2 to 3 pancakes with cottage cheese, leaving top pancake plain. Serve with any of the fruit sauces on pages 42 and 43.

# surprise muffins

**1-1/4 cups regular all-purpose flour**
**3 teaspoons baking powder**
**1 teaspoon salt**
**1/3 cup sugar**
**2 cups Corn Flakes cereal**
**1 cup milk**
**1 egg**
**1/3 cup shortening**
**1/4 cup preserves or jam**

- Stir together flour, baking powder, salt and sugar. Set aside.

- Measure Corn Flakes cereal into large mixing bowl. Stir in milk. Let stand 2 to 3 minutes or until cereal is softened. Add egg and shortening. Beat well. Add flour mixture, stirring only until combined. Portion batter evenly into 12 greased 2-1/2-inch muffin-pan cups.

- Make a deep indentation in top of batter for each muffin. Fill each with measuring-teaspoon of preserves.

- Bake in oven at 400° F. about 25 minutes or until golden brown. Serve warm with whipped cream cheese, if desired.

Yield:  12 muffins

# bran muffins

1-1/4 cups regular all-purpose flour

   3 teaspoons baking powder

 1/2 teaspoon salt

 1/2 cup sugar

1-1/2 cups All-Bran cereal or Bran Buds cereal

1-1/4 cups milk

    1 egg

 1/3 cup shortening or vegetable oil

- Stir together flour, baking powder, salt and sugar. Set aside.

- Measure All-Bran cereal and milk into large mixing bowl. Stir to combine. Let stand 1 to 2 minutes or until cereal is softened. Add egg and shortening. Beat well.

- Add flour mixture, stirring only until combined. Portion batter evenly into 12 greased 2-1/2-inch muffin-pan cups.

- Bake in oven at 400° F. about 25 minutes or until lightly browned.

Yield:   12 muffins

## VARIATIONS:

3 cups Raisin Bran cereal or 2-1/2 cups 40% Bran Flakes cereal may be substituted for the All-Bran cereal.

# brancakes

1-1/2 cups regular all-purpose flour

   3 teaspoons baking powder

 3/4 teaspoon salt

   2 tablespoons sugar

   1 egg

   2 cups milk

   2 tablespoons vegetable oil

   1 teaspoon grated orange peel (optional)

   1 cup All-Bran cereal or Bran Buds cereal

- Stir together flour, baking powder, salt and sugar. Set aside.

- In large mixing bowl, beat egg until foamy. Stir in milk, oil, orange peel and All-Bran cereal. Let stand 1 to 2 minutes or until cereal is softened. Add flour mixture, stirring to combine. Batter will be lumpy.

- Dip up batter, using 1/4 cup for each pancake. Cook on greased and preheated griddle, turning once, until golden brown on both sides. Serve with warm pancake syrup or *Fresh Orange Syrup* (see page 42).

Yield:   14 pancakes

# crumbs-topped coffee cake

**1/2 cup Corn Flake Crumbs**

**1/4 cup sugar**

**1/2 teaspoon ground cinnamon**

    **2 tablespoons regular margarine or butter, softened**

    \*      \*      \*      \*      \*

    **1 cup regular all-purpose flour**

    **3 teaspoons baking powder**

**1/2 teaspoon salt**

**1/4 cup sugar**

    **1 cup Corn Flake Crumbs**

    **1 cup milk**

    **1 egg**

**1/4 cup shortening**

- For topping, measure first 4 ingredients into small mixing bowl. Mix until well combined. Set aside.

- Stir together flour, baking powder, salt and sugar. Set aside.

- Combine the 1 cup Corn Flake Crumbs, the milk, egg and shortening in large mixing bowl. Beat well. Add flour mixture, stirring only until combined. Spread batter evenly in greased 8 x 8 x 2-inch baking pan. Sprinkle topping over batter, pressing in gently.

- Bake in oven at 400° F. about 25 minutes or until wooden pick inserted near center comes out clean. Cut into squares. Serve warm.

Yield:   9 servings

# bran cherry nut bread

2 cups regular all-purpose flour
3 teaspoons baking powder
1 teaspoon salt
1/2 teaspoon ground nutmeg
3/4 cup sugar
1-1/2 cups All-Bran cereal or Bran Buds cereal
1-1/4 cups milk
1 egg
2 tablespoons vegetable oil or shortening
1 jar (10 oz.) maraschino cherries, drained and finely chopped
3/4 cup chopped walnuts

    *     *     *     *     *

1 tablespoon regular margarine or butter
1/4 cup sugar
1/4 cup chopped walnuts

- Stir together flour, baking powder, salt, nutmeg and the 3/4 cup sugar. Set aside.

- Measure All-Bran cereal and milk into large mixing bowl. Stir to combine. Let stand 1 to 2 minutes or until cereal is softened. Add egg and oil. Beat well.

- Add flour mixture, stirring only until combined. Reserve 2 tablespoons chopped cherries for topping. Fold remaining cherries and the 3/4 cup walnuts into batter. Spread batter evenly in greased 9 x 5 x 3-inch loaf pan. Set aside.

- For topping, measure margarine into small frypan. Cook over low heat until bubbly. Remove from heat. Stir in the 1/4 cup sugar, the 1/4 cup walnuts and the reserved 2 tablespoons cherries. Sprinkle over batter.

- Bake in oven at 350° F. about 1 hour or until wooden pick inserted near center comes out clean. Let cool 10 minutes before removing from pan. Cool completely on wire rack before slicing.

Yield:  1 loaf

**VARIATION:**

**Cracklin' Bran Cherry Nut Bread:** Reduce sugar from 3/4 cup to 1/2 cup. Substitute 1-1/2 cups Cracklin' Bran cereal for the All-Bran cereal. In step 2, let cereal and milk mixture stand about 10 minutes or until cereal is softened. Continue as directed on page 38.

# pumpkin nut bread

1-1/2 cups regular all-purpose flour
2 teaspoons baking powder
1/2 teaspoon baking soda
1/2 teaspoon salt
1 teaspoon ground cinnamon
1/2 teaspoon ground cloves
1/4 teaspoon ground ginger
1/4 teaspoon ground allspice
1/4 cup regular margarine or butter, softened
1/2 cup sugar
1 egg
1/2 cup milk
1 teaspoon vanilla flavoring
1 cup solid pack pumpkin
1 cup All-Bran cereal or Bran Buds cereal
1/2 cup chopped nuts

- In small mixing bowl, stir together flour, baking powder, soda, salt and spices. Set aside.

- In large mixing bowl, beat margarine and sugar until well blended. Add egg, milk and vanilla. Beat well. Stir in pumpkin, All-Bran cereal and nuts. Add flour mixture. Mix until well combined. Spread batter evenly in well-greased 9 x 5 x 3-inch loaf pan.

- Bake in oven at 350° F. about 50 minutes or until wooden pick inserted near center comes out clean. Remove from pan. Cool completely on wire rack before slicing. Serve half slices sandwich-style with softened cream cheese as the filling, if desired.

Yield: 1 loaf

NOTE: 1 cup pumpkin is half of a 1 lb. can. Remainder can be frozen.

# marmalade coffee cake

1 cup regular all-purpose flour
2-1/2 teaspoons baking powder
1/2 teaspoon salt
1/4 cup sugar
1-1/2 cups 40% Bran Flakes cereal
3/4 cup milk
1 egg
1/4 cup shortening
1/2 cup orange marmalade

- Stir together flour, baking powder, salt and sugar. Set aside.

- Measure 40% Bran Flakes cereal and milk into large mixing bowl. Stir to combine. Let stand 1 to 2 minutes or until cereal is softened. Add egg and shortening. Beat well. Add flour mixture, stirring only until combined. Spread in greased 9 x 9 x 2-inch baking pan. Top with marmalade, spreading evenly over batter.

- Bake in oven at 400° F. about 30 minutes or until golden brown. Cut into squares. Serve warm.

Yield: 9 servings

**VARIATION:**

Other fruit preserves may be used in place of orange marmalade.

# baked French toast

3/4 cup Corn Flake Crumbs
2 eggs
3/4 cup milk
1/2 teaspoon vanilla flavoring
6 slices day-old bread, cut into halves diagonally
1/4 cup regular margarine or butter, melted

- Measure Corn Flake Crumbs into shallow dish or pan. Set aside.

- In a second shallow dish or pan, beat eggs until foamy. Stir in milk and vanilla. Dip bread into egg mixture, turning once and allowing time for both sides to take up liquid. Coat evenly with Crumbs. Place in single layer on well-greased baking sheet. Drizzle with melted margarine.

- Bake in oven at 450° F. about 10 minutes or until lightly browned. Serve with warm maple syrup, jelly or honey.

Yield:   4 servings, 3 halves each

# pineapple crisp coffee cake

**1-1/2 cups Sugar Frosted Flakes of Corn cereal**
**1 tablespoon regular margarine or butter, melted**

*          *          *          *          *

**1-1/2 cups regular all-purpose flour**
**2 teaspoons baking powder**
**1/2 teaspoon salt**
**1/4 cup regular margarine or butter, softened**
**3/4 cup sugar**
**1 egg**
**Water**
**1 can (8-1/4 oz.) crushed pineapple, well drained, reserving syrup**
**1/4 cup flaked coconut**

- Crush the 1-1/2 cups Sugar Frosted Flakes of Corn cereal to measure 3/4 cup. Combine with the 1 tablespoon melted margarine, stirring until well coated. Set aside.

- Stir together flour, baking powder and salt. Set aside.

- In large mixing bowl, beat the 1/4 cup margarine and the sugar until well blended. Add egg. Beat well. Add water, if necessary, to reserved pineapple syrup to measure 1/2 cup. Stir into egg mixture. Add flour mixture. Mix thoroughly. Spread batter evenly in greased 9-inch round cake pan. Sprinkle coconut and pineapple evenly over batter. Top with cereal mixture, pressing gently into batter.

- Bake in oven at 350° F. about 50 minutes or until wooden pick inserted near center comes out clean. Cool 5 minutes. Cut into wedges. Serve warm.

Yield:   8 servings

# quick 'n delicious toppings for waffles

- Heat Eggo Frozen Waffles according to package directions in a toaster or oven. Then serve with any of the following toppings:

  Warm maple or fruit syrup

  Honey or honey butter

  Jam, jelly or preserves

  Melted margarine or butter and a sprinkle of sugar and ground cinnamon

  Whipped cream cheese

  Orange marmalade or other fruit preserves folded into whipped cream cheese

  Sliced bananas, chopped nuts and warm maple syrup

  Blueberries, raspberries, peaches or strawberries mixed with sour cream, with a sprinkle of brown sugar on top

  Eggs scrambled with cubed ham, chopped green pepper and onions

  Canadian bacon or a thin slice of ham topped with hot raisin, pineapple or cherry sauce

# fresh orange syrup

**1 cup sugar**

**Dash salt**

**1 teaspoon grated orange peel**

**2 teaspoons cornstarch**

**1/2 cup orange juice**

**1/4 cup regular margarine or butter**

**1 sectioned orange, with seeds and membranes removed**

- Stir together sugar, salt, orange peel and cornstarch in small saucepan. Gradually stir in orange juice. Add margarine. Bring to boil and cook, stirring constantly, until thickened and clear. Remove from heat. Stir in orange sections. Serve warm or cooled.

Yield:  1-2/3 cups

# fresh strawberry sauce

      **1 pint fresh strawberries**
  **1/3 cup sugar**

● Wash, hull and slice strawberries. Place in small mixing bowl. Stir in sugar. Let stand at room temperature 1 to 2 hours.

Yield:  1-1/2 cups


# blueberry peach sauce

      **1 tablespoon cornstarch**
  **1/2 cup cold water**
      **1 package (10 oz.) frozen blueberries, thawed**
      **1 package (10 oz.) frozen peaches, thawed**

● Dissolve cornstarch in water in medium-size saucepan. Stir in fruit. Bring to boil and cook, stirring constantly, until thickened and clear. Serve warm.

Yield:  3 cups


# apricot sauce

      **1 jar (12 oz.) apricot jam**
  **2/3 cup water**

● Stir together jam and water in small saucepan. Cook over medium heat, stirring constantly, until jam is melted and sauce is smooth. Serve warm or cooled.

Yield:  1-1/2 cups

# molasses brown bread

        1 cup regular all-purpose flour
        1 teaspoon baking soda
    1/2 teaspoon salt
    1/2 teaspoon ground cinnamon
        1 egg
        1 cup All-Bran cereal or Bran Buds cereal
    1/2 cup seedless raisins
        2 tablespoons shortening
    1/3 cup molasses
    3/4 cup very hot water

● Stir together flour, soda, salt and cinnamon. Set aside.

● In large mixing bowl, beat egg slightly. Mix in All-Bran cereal, raisins, shortening and molasses. Add water, stirring until shortening is melted. Add flour mixture, stirring only until combined. Fill 2 greased metal cans, 4-1/4 inches deep and 3 inches across, about two-thirds full.

● Bake in oven at 350° F. about 45 minutes or until wooden pick inserted near center comes out clean. Remove from cans. Let cool slightly. Slice and serve warm. Or cool completely on wire rack, wrap tightly and store overnight.

Yield:   2 loaves, 4-1/4 x 3 inches

See page 184 for microwave directions.

# curried bran biscuits

    1/2 cup All-Bran cereal or Bran Buds cereal
    2/3 cup milk
1-1/3 cups regular all-purpose flour
2-1/2 teaspoons baking powder
        1 teaspoon salt
    1/4 teaspoon curry powder
    1/3 cup shortening

- Measure All-Bran cereal and milk into small mixing bowl. Stir to combine. Let stand 1 to 2 minutes or until cereal is softened.

- In large mixing bowl, stir together flour, baking powder, salt and curry powder. Cut in shortening until mixture resembles coarse meal. Add cereal mixture, stirring only until combined.

- On lightly floured surface, gently knead dough a few times. Roll out to 3/4-inch thickness. Cut with floured 1-3/4-inch biscuit cutter into 12 biscuits. Place on ungreased baking sheet.

- Bake in oven at 425° F. about 10 minutes or until lightly browned. Serve immediately. Or split hot biscuits and serve with *Deluxe Creamed Turkey* (see page 127).

Yield:   12 biscuits

# bran 'n molasses muffins

1-1/4 **cups regular all-purpose flour**
1 **teaspoon baking powder**
1/2 **teaspoon baking soda**
1 **teaspoon salt**
1 **cup All-Bran cereal or Bran Buds cereal**
3/4 **cup milk**
1/2 **cup molasses**
1 **egg**
1/3 **cup shortening**
1/2 **cup seedless raisins**

- Stir together flour, baking powder, soda and salt. Set aside.

- Measure All-Bran cereal, milk and molasses into large mixing bowl. Stir to combine. Let stand 1 to 2 minutes or until cereal is softened. Add egg and shortening. Beat well. Stir in raisins.

- Add flour mixture, stirring only until combined. Portion batter evenly into 12 greased 2-1/2-inch muffin-pan cups.

- Bake in oven at 400° F. about 15 minutes or until golden brown.

Yield:   12 muffins

# YEAST BREADS

# YEAST BREADS

If there is one aroma from your childhood you've never forgotten, it is probably that delectable fragrance of freshly baked bread. Homemade yeast bread has a melt-in-your-mouth goodness and unforgettable flavor that can't be beat!

1. cranberry-filled coffee cake, p. 55
2. anadama bread, p. 52
3. hot roll bran bread, p. 61
4. save-a-day rolls, p. 62
5. cinnamon easy's, p. 58
6. date-filled tea ring, p. 57
7. delicious cinnamon twists, p. 60

# cinnamon swirl bread

2 cups Sugar Frosted Flakes of Corn cereal
5 to 5-1/2 cups regular all-purpose flour
2 packages active dry yeast
1 tablespoon salt
2 cups warm water (110° to 115° F.)
1 egg
1/4 cup vegetable oil

*       *       *       *       *

1 cup Sugar Frosted Flakes of Corn cereal
1/4 cup firmly packed brown sugar
2 teaspoons ground cinnamon
2 tablespoons regular margarine or butter, melted
Confectioners' Sugar Glaze (see page 151)

- Crush the 2 cups Sugar Frosted Flakes of Corn cereal to measure 1 cup. In large bowl of electric mixer, stir together the crushed cereal, 3 cups of the flour, the yeast and salt. Add warm water, egg and oil. Beat 3 minutes at medium speed. By hand, gradually stir in enough remaining flour to make a stiff dough.

- On lightly floured surface, knead dough about 5 minutes or until smooth and elastic. Place in greased bowl, turning once to grease top. Cover lightly. Let rise in warm place until double in volume (about 1-1/2 hours).

- Meanwhile, crush the remaining 1 cup Sugar Frosted Flakes of Corn cereal to fine crumbs. Combine with brown sugar, cinnamon and margarine. Set aside.

- Punch down dough. Divide in half. On lightly floured surface, roll or pat each half to a 14 x 7-inch rectangle. Sprinkle each with cereal mixture. Starting with shorter side, roll up tightly, pressing dough into roll with each turn. Pinch edges and ends to seal. Place in 2 greased 9 x 5 x 3-inch loaf pans. Cover and let rise in warm place until double in volume (about 45 minutes).

- Bake in oven at 375° F. about 40 minutes or until golden brown. Remove from pans. Place on wire racks. Drizzle with *Confectioners' Sugar Glaze* or brush with additional melted margarine, if desired.

Yield:   2 loaves

# whole wheat bran bread

1 cup regular all-purpose flour

1 cup whole wheat flour

1 cup All-Bran cereal or Bran Buds cereal

1 tablespoon sugar

1 teaspoon salt

1 package active dry yeast

3/4 cup milk

1 tablespoon molasses

3 tablespoons regular margarine or butter

1 egg

1 tablespoon regular margarine or butter, melted

- In small mixing bowl, stir together regular all-purpose flour and whole wheat flour. In large bowl of electric mixer, combine 1/2 cup of the flour mixture, the All-Bran cereal, sugar, salt and yeast. Set aside.

- In small saucepan, combine milk, molasses and the 3 tablespoons margarine. Place over low heat until very warm (120° to 130° F.). Remove from heat. Gradually add to cereal mixture and beat at medium speed on electric mixer for 2 minutes, scraping bowl occasionally.

- Add egg and 1/4 cup of the flour mixture. Beat at high speed on electric mixer for 2 minutes. With spoon, stir in remaining flour mixture to make a stiff dough. On lightly floured surface, knead dough about 5 minutes or until smooth and elastic. Place in greased bowl, turning once to grease top. Cover lightly. Let rise in warm place until double in volume (about 1 hour).

- Punch down dough. Shape into smooth round ball, being careful not to make large folds in dough. Place on greased baking sheet. Cover and let rise in warm place until double in volume (about 1 hour).

- Bake on center rack of oven at 375° F. about 25 minutes or until golden brown. Immediately remove from baking sheet. Place on wire rack. Brush with melted margarine.

Yield:   1 loaf

# no-knead bran bread

3 cups regular all-purpose flour

1/2 cup instant nonfat dry milk (in dry form)

1-1/2 teaspoons salt

2 packages active dry yeast

1/4 cup sugar

1-1/2 cups warm water (110° to 115° F.)

2 cups All-Bran cereal or Bran Buds cereal

1 egg

1/3 cup regular margarine or butter, softened

1 tablespoon regular margarine or butter, melted

- Stir together flour, nonfat dry milk and salt. Set aside.

- Combine yeast, sugar and warm water in large bowl of electric mixer. Stir in All-Bran cereal. Let stand about 2 minutes or until cereal is softened.

- Add egg, margarine and about half the flour mixture. Beat at medium speed on electric mixer for 2 minutes or about 200 strokes by hand. Mix in remaining flour mixture by hand to form a stiff, sticky dough.

- Cover lightly. Let rise in warm place until double in volume (about 1 hour). Stir down dough to original volume. Spoon into well-greased 9 x 5 x 3-inch loaf pan.

- Bake in oven at 375° F. about 45 minutes or until loaf sounds hollow when lightly tapped. Immediately remove from pan. Place on wire rack. Brush with melted margarine.

Yield:  1 loaf

**VARIATION:**

**No-Knead Raisin Bread:**  In step 1, stir 1/2 teaspoon ground cinnamon into flour mixture. In step 4, add 1 cup seedless raisins, stirring dough down to original volume. Before baking, brush top of loaf with the 1 tablespoon melted margarine. Sprinkle with a mixture of 1/2 teaspoon ground cinnamon and 2 tablespoons sugar. Then bake as directed in step 5.

# anadama bread

1-1/2 cups boiling water
1 cup Corn Flake Crumbs
1/2 cup molasses
1/3 cup shortening
1 tablespoon salt
4 to 4-1/2 cups regular all-purpose flour
2 packages active dry yeast
1 egg
2 tablespoons regular margarine or butter, melted

- Measure water and Corn Flake Crumbs into medium-size mixing bowl. Stir in molasses, shortening and salt. Let stand until lukewarm.

- Stir together 1 cup of the flour and the yeast. Add Crumbs mixture and egg. Beat well.

- Stir in enough remaining flour to make a stiff dough. On lightly floured surface, knead dough about 8 minutes or until smooth and elastic. Place in greased bowl, turning once to grease top. Cover lightly. Let rise in warm place until double in volume (about 1 hour).

- Punch down dough. Divide in half. Cover and let rest 10 minutes. Shape each half into round, slightly flattened loaf. Place loaves in opposite corners of baking sheet. Cover and let rise in warm place until almost double (about 45 minutes).

- Bake in oven at 375° F. for 20 minutes. Cover with foil to prevent over-browning and continue baking about 20 minutes longer. Remove from baking sheet. Place on wire rack. Brush with melted margarine.

Yield:  2 loaves

# caraway rye bran bread

1 cup buttermilk

1 package active dry yeast

1/4 cup warm water (110° to 115° F.)

1/4 cup sugar

3/4 teaspoon salt

1 teaspoon grated orange peel

1 teaspoon caraway seed

2 cups 40% Bran Flakes cereal

1 cup rye flour

1-1/2 cups regular all-purpose flour

1 tablespoon milk

- Measure buttermilk. Let stand until it reaches room temperature.

- Dissolve yeast in warm water in large mixing bowl. Stir in sugar, salt, orange peel, caraway seed and warm buttermilk. Stir in 40% Bran Flakes cereal and rye flour. Gradually mix in all-purpose flour. If necessary, work in last portion of flour while kneading. Cover and let rest 15 minutes.

- On lightly floured surface, knead dough about 5 minutes or until smooth and elastic. Place in greased bowl, turning once to grease top. Cover lightly. Let rise in warm place until double in volume (about 1-1/2 hours).

- Sprinkle small amount of cornmeal on baking sheet or grease lightly. Punch down dough. Shape into smooth round ball, being careful not to make large folds in dough. Place on baking sheet. Flatten slightly. Cut large X across top of loaf with sharp knife. Cover and let rise in warm place until double in volume (about 45 minutes). Brush loaf with milk.

- Bake in oven at 350° F. about 35 minutes or until golden brown and loaf sounds hollow when tapped. Remove from baking sheet. Cool on wire rack.

Yield:   1 loaf

## VARIATIONS:

1 cup All-Bran cereal or Bran Buds cereal may be substituted for the 40% Bran Flakes cereal.

# bran walnut roll-ups

1 package active dry yeast

1/3 cup warm water (110° to 115° F.)

1-1/2 cups regular all-purpose flour

1/8 teaspoon salt

1 tablespoon granulated sugar

1 egg

1 cup 40% Bran Flakes cereal

1/2 cup regular margarine or butter, softened

*        *        *        *        *

1 package (3 oz.) cream cheese, softened

1/4 cup granulated sugar

2 teaspoons grated lemon peel

1/2 cup finely chopped walnuts

Confectioners' sugar

- Dissolve yeast in warm water. Set aside.

- Stir together flour, salt and the 1 tablespoon granulated sugar. Set aside.

- In large mixing bowl, beat egg slightly. Stir in yeast mixture and 40% Bran Flakes cereal. Add margarine. Beat well. Mix in flour mixture. Cover lightly. Let rise in warm place until double in volume (about 1 hour).

- Stir down dough. Divide in half. On lightly floured surface, roll out each half to an 11 x 7-inch rectangle.

- Place cream cheese, the 1/4 cup granulated sugar and the lemon peel in small mixing bowl. Beat until light and fluffy. Spread half the mixture over each rectangle. Sprinkle with walnuts.

- Starting from long side, roll up dough like a jelly roll. Place rolls, seam side down, on lightly greased baking sheet. Slit each roll halfway through lengthwise.

- Bake in oven at 375° F. about 25 minutes or until lightly browned. Remove from oven. Cool. Sprinkle with confectioners' sugar. Cut into diagonal pieces to serve.

Yield:   2 rolls, 12 slices each

# cranberry-filled coffee cake

    1 cup cranberries
1/2 cup sugar

        *      *      *      *      *

    1 package active dry yeast
1/4 cup warm water (110° to 115° F.)
1/2 cup milk
    3 tablespoons shortening
1/2 cup Corn Flake Crumbs
1/2 teaspoon salt
1/4 cup sugar
2-1/4 cups regular all-purpose flour
    1 egg, slightly beaten
      Confectioners' Sugar Glaze (see page 151)
      Chopped nuts (optional)

- Measure cranberries and the 1/2 cup sugar into small saucepan. Cook over low heat, stirring constantly, until sugar is dissolved and cranberry skins are broken. Set aside for filling.

- Dissolve yeast in warm water. Set aside.

- Scald milk. Remove from heat. Pour into large mixing bowl. Add shortening, Corn Flake Crumbs, salt and the 1/4 cup sugar, mixing until well combined. Let stand until lukewarm.

- Stir in enough flour to make a thick batter (about 1 cup). Add yeast mixture and egg. Beat well. Stir in enough remaining flour to make a soft dough.

- On lightly floured surface, knead dough about 10 minutes or until smooth and elastic. Place in greased bowl, turning once to grease top. Cover lightly. Let rise in warm place until double in volume (about 1 hour).

- Punch down dough. On lightly floured surface, roll dough to 12 x 9-inch rectangle. Spread cranberry filling lengthwise over half the dough. Fold other half of dough over filling, pressing edges together. Place on greased baking sheet. Let rise in warm place until double in volume (about 30 minutes).

- Bake in oven at 350° F. about 20 minutes or until golden brown. Remove from oven. Place on wire rack. Drizzle with *Confectioners' Sugar Glaze*. Sprinkle with chopped nuts, if desired.

Yield: 8 servings

# three-way yeast breads

        2 packages active dry yeast
    1/2 cup warm water (110° to 115° F.)
    3/4 cup shortening
        2 cups All-Bran cereal or Bran Buds cereal
        2 teaspoons salt
    3/4 cup sugar
  1-1/2 cups boiling water
        2 eggs, slightly beaten
        6 cups regular all-purpose flour

- Dissolve yeast in warm water. Set aside.

- Measure shortening, All-Bran cereal, salt and sugar into large mixing bowl. Add boiling water, stirring until shortening is melted. Let stand until lukewarm.

- Stir in eggs and yeast mixture. Add half the flour. Mix well. Add remaining flour. Stir until well combined. Place in greased bowl, turning once to grease top. Cover lightly. Let rise in warm place until double in volume (about 1 hour).

- Punch down dough. Use to make *Caramel Rolls, Date-Filled Tea Ring* or *Dinner Rolls.* Or cover bowl tightly and store in refrigerator until needed.

# caramel rolls

        Three-Way Yeast Breads dough (see above)
        5 tablespoons regular margarine or butter, melted
    1/2 cup dark corn syrup

- Use one-third of the prepared dough. If refrigerated, allow dough to reach room temperature before shaping.

- Measure 1 teaspoon melted margarine and 2 teaspoons corn syrup into each of 12 greased 2-1/2-inch muffin-pan cups. Shape dough into 12 smooth balls. Place in muffin-pan cups. Brush tops with remaining melted margarine. Let rise in warm place until double in volume (about 1 hour).

- Bake in oven at 425° F. about 15 minutes or until lightly browned. Remove from oven. Invert onto serving plate. Serve warm.

Yield:   12 rolls

# date-filled tea ring

**Three-Way Yeast Breads dough (see page 56)**
**1 package (8 oz.) pitted dates**
**1/2 cup water**
**1/2 cup sugar**
**2 tablespoons regular margarine or butter, melted**
**Confectioners' Sugar Glaze (see page 151)**

- Use one-third of the prepared dough. If refrigerated, allow dough to reach room temperature before shaping.

- In small saucepan, combine dates, water and sugar. Cook over low heat, stirring occasionally, until smooth and thickened. Remove from heat. Set aside to cool.

- On lightly floured surface, roll dough to 18 x 6-inch rectangle. Brush with melted margarine. Spread with date mixture. Starting from long side, roll up dough like a jelly roll. Seal edge. Place roll on greased baking sheet, shaping into ring and pressing 2 ends tightly together. With scissors, cut from outside edge toward center at 1-inch intervals. Twist each section slightly so cut edge is up. Cover lightly. Let rise in warm place until double in volume (about 1 hour).

- Bake in oven at 375° F. about 25 minutes or until lightly browned. Remove from oven. Drizzle with *Confectioners' Sugar Glaze.* Serve warm.

Yield:   12 servings

# dinner rolls

**Three-Way Yeast Breads dough (see page 56)**
**1 tablespoon melted margarine or butter**
**Poppy seed or sesame seed**

- Use one-third of the prepared dough. If refrigerated, allow dough to reach room temperature before shaping.

- Shape dough into 8 smooth balls. Place on greased baking sheet. Let rise in warm place until double in volume (about 1 hour).

- Brush tops with melted margarine. Sprinkle with poppy seed. Bake in oven at 375° F. about 15 minutes or until lightly browned. Serve warm.

Yield:   8 rolls

# cinnamon easy's

3 tablespoons regular margarine or butter, melted
2/3 cup firmly packed brown sugar
1/2 cup dark corn syrup
1/2 cup pecan halves

*      *      *      *      *

1 teaspoon ground cinnamon
1/4 cup firmly packed brown sugar

*      *      *      *      *

2 packages active dry yeast
1-1/4 cups warm water (110° to 115° F.)
1-1/2 cups Raisin Bran cereal
6 tablespoons regular margarine or butter, softened
1 teaspoon salt
1 package (3 oz.) egg custard mix
3 to 3-1/2 cups regular all-purpose flour

- Combine first 4 ingredients in greased 13 x 9 x 2-inch baking pan. Spread evenly. Set aside. Stir together cinnamon and the 1/4 cup sugar. Set aside.

- Dissolve yeast in warm water in large mixing bowl. Add Raisin Bran cereal. Let stand about 2 minutes or until cereal is softened. Add 4 table-spoons of the softened margarine, the salt and custard mix, stirring until mix is dissolved. Stir in enough flour to make a stiff dough.

- On lightly floured surface, knead dough into an 18 x 12-inch rectangle. Spread the remaining 2 tablespoons softened margarine over dough. Sprinkle with cinnamon-sugar mixture. Starting from shorter side, roll up dough like a jelly roll. Seal edge. Cut into 1-inch slices. Place cut side down on pecan mixture in pan. Let rise in warm place until double in volume (about 1 hour).

- Bake in oven at 400° F. about 25 minutes or until lightly browned. Remove from oven. Invert onto serving plate. Serve warm.

Yield:  12 rolls

**VARIATIONS:**

1/2 cup All-Bran cereal or Bran Buds cereal may be substituted for the Raisin Bran cereal.

# bran English muffins

1 cup milk

2 tablespoons regular margarine or butter

1 teaspoon salt

3/4 cup All-Bran cereal or Bran Buds cereal

1 package active dry yeast

1/4 cup warm water (110° to 115° F.)

2-3/4 cups regular all-purpose flour

- Measure milk, margarine and salt into medium-size saucepan. Cook over low heat, stirring frequently, until margarine melts. Remove from heat. Stir in All-Bran cereal. Let stand until lukewarm.

- In large mixing bowl, dissolve yeast in warm water. Stir in cereal mixture. Gradually add 2-1/2 cups of the flour, mixing until dough leaves sides of bowl.

- On flat surface sprinkled with remaining 1/4 cup flour, knead dough about 5 minutes or until smooth and elastic. Add more flour if dough becomes sticky. Place in greased bowl, turning once to grease top. Cover lightly. Let rise in warm place until double in volume (about 45 minutes).

- Punch down dough. On lightly floured surface, roll out to 1/2-inch thickness. Cut with floured 3-inch biscuit cutter into 12 muffins. Cover and let rise in warm place until double in volume (about 45 minutes).

- Preheat electric frypan to 250° F. or preheat regular large frypan over low heat. Place muffins in ungreased frypan. Cook uncovered about 25 minutes, turning once, or until lightly browned on both sides. Cool completely. Split and toast muffins to serve.

Yield:   12 muffins

NOTE:  For softer crust, refrigerate muffins in tightly covered container overnight before serving.

# delicious cinnamon twists

  1-1/2 cups Sugar Frosted Flakes of Corn cereal
    1/3 cup chopped nuts
    1/4 cup sugar
      1 teaspoon ground cinnamon

        *         *         *         *         *

      2 packages active dry yeast
    1/4 cup warm water (110° to 115° F.)
    1/2 cup milk
    1/2 cup shortening
      3 tablespoons sugar
  1-1/2 teaspoons salt
      1 teaspoon vanilla flavoring
      3 cups regular all-purpose flour
      3 eggs
    1/4 cup regular margarine or butter, melted

● Crush the 1-1/2 cups Sugar Frosted Flakes of Corn cereal to fine crumbs. Place in shallow dish or pan. Stir in nuts, the 1/4 cup sugar and the cinnamon. Set aside.

● Dissolve yeast in warm water. Set aside.

● Scald milk. Remove from heat. Pour into large mixing bowl. Add shortening, the 3 tablespoons sugar, the salt and vanilla, stirring until shortening is melted. Let stand until lukewarm.

● Stir in yeast mixture. Add half the flour, mixing until smooth. Add eggs, one at a time, beating well after each addition. Add remaining flour to make a soft dough. Mix until well combined. Cover lightly. Let rise in warm place until double in volume (about 30 minutes).

● Stir down dough. On lightly floured surface, divide into 16 pieces. With fingers, gently roll each piece to make a 6-inch stick. Dip in melted margarine. Coat with cereal mixture, twisting stick slightly. Place on ungreased baking sheet.

● Bake in oven at 375° F. about 15 minutes or until lightly browned.

Yield:   16 twists

# hot roll bran bread

    1 cup All-Bran cereal or Bran Buds cereal
1/4 cup wheat germ
1/2 teaspoon salt
    1 tablespoon regular margarine or butter
    1 tablespoon honey
1/2 cup boiling water
    1 package (13-3/4 oz.) hot roll mix
3/4 cup warm water (110° to 115° F.)
    2 eggs

- In large mixing bowl, combine All-Bran cereal, wheat germ, salt, margarine, honey and boiling water. Let stand until lukewarm.

- Dissolve yeast from hot roll mix in warm water. Add yeast mixture, eggs and packaged flour mixture to cereal mixture. Beat well. Cover lightly. Let rise in warm place until double in volume (30 to 40 minutes).

- Stir down dough. Spoon into well-greased 9 x 5 x 3-inch loaf pan. Cover and let rise in warm place until double in volume (30 to 40 minutes).

- Bake in oven at 375° F. about 40 minutes or until deep golden brown. If loaf becomes too brown, cover with foil during last 10 minutes of baking. Immediately remove from pan. Cool on wire rack.

Yield:  1 loaf

## VARIATIONS:

1-1/2 cups Raisin Bran cereal or 1 cup 40% Bran Flakes cereal may be substituted for the All-Bran cereal.

# save-a-day rolls

2 packages active dry yeast
1 cup warm water (110° to 115° F.)
1 cup shortening
3/4 cup sugar
2 cups All-Bran cereal or Bran Buds cereal
2 teaspoons salt
1 cup boiling water
6 cups regular all-purpose flour
2 eggs, slightly beaten

- Dissolve yeast in warm water. Set aside.

- Measure shortening, sugar, All-Bran cereal and salt into large mixing bowl. Add boiling water. Stir until shortening is melted. Let stand until lukewarm.

- Mix half the flour into cereal mixture. Stir in yeast mixture and eggs. Mix in remaining flour. Refrigerate, tightly covered, overnight and use as needed. May be stored 2 to 3 days.

- Remove dough from refrigerator 1 hour before shaping rolls. Punch down. Place three 1-inch balls of dough in greased 2-1/2-inch muffin-pan cups. Cover and let rise in warm place until double in volume (about 1 hour).

- Bake in oven at 425° F. about 12 minutes or until browned.

Yield:   36 rolls


# honey buns

1/2 cup milk
2 tablespoons sugar
1/2 teaspoon salt
2 tablespoons regular margarine or butter, softened
1-1/2 cups Corn Flakes cereal
1 package active dry yeast
1-3/4 cups regular all-purpose flour
1 egg
1/4 cup seedless raisins

**1 tablespoon regular margarine or butter, melted**

**2 tablespoons sugar**

**1/2 teaspoon ground cinnamon**

\*　　　\*　　　\*　　　\*　　　\*

**2 tablespoons regular margarine or butter**

**1/4 cup honey**

**2 tablespoons sugar**

**1/4 cup chopped nuts**

● Scald milk. Remove from heat. Stir in 2 tablespoons sugar, the salt and 2 tablespoons margarine. Cool to lukewarm.

● Meanwhile, stir together Corn Flakes cereal, undissolved dry yeast and 3/4 cup of the flour. Add to lukewarm milk mixture. Mix well. Add egg. Beat well. Stir in raisins. Gradually add remaining flour to form a soft dough, mixing well. Place in greased bowl, turning once to grease top. Cover lightly. Let rise in warm place until double in volume (1-1/2 to 2 hours).

● Punch down dough. On lightly floured surface, roll dough to a 16 x 8-inch rectangle. Brush with 1 tablespoon melted margarine. Sprinkle with a mixture of 2 tablespoons sugar and the cinnamon. Starting from shorter side, roll up like a jelly roll. Seal edge. Cut into eight slices. Set aside.

● For honey topping, melt 2 tablespoons margarine. Stir in honey, 2 table-spoons sugar and the nuts. Spread evenly in 8-inch round cake pan. Ar-range rolls, cut side down, over honey mixture.

● Cover and let rise in warm place until double in volume (30 to 40 minutes). Bake in oven at 375° F. about 20 minutes or until lightly browned. Remove from oven. Invert onto serving plate. Serve warm.

Yield:　8 rolls

# VEGETABLES, SALADS & SIDE DISHES

# VEGETABLES, SALADS & SIDE DISHES

Go creative and add pizazz to any lunch or dinner with a unique vegetable, perky salad or outstanding side dish. Easy-to-prepare meal accompaniments add just the right touch to help make every meal "special."

1. quick herbed tomatoes, p. 75
2. tossed salad deluxe, p. 67
3. crispy potato balls, p. 82
4. Hawaiian stuffing, p. 71
5. savory bran-rice pilaf, p. 76
6. herbed zucchini bake, p. 81
7. stuffin' muffins, p. 83
8. crunchy bran topping for soup, p. 73
9. fettuccini, p. 80

# tossed salad deluxe

**1/4 cup regular margarine or butter**

**1/8 teaspoon garlic powder**

**1 tablespoon sesame seed**

**2 cups Croutettes herb seasoned croutons**

**1 quart romaine or iceberg lettuce, torn into bite-size pieces**

**1 quart spinach leaves, torn into bite-size pieces**

**1/2 cup small sweet onion rings**

**1 teaspoon salt**

**1/4 teaspoon pepper**

**1/2 teaspoon dry mustard**

**3 tablespoons vinegar**

**1 tablespoon honey**

**1/2 cup vegetable oil**

**3 medium-size tomatoes, cut into wedges**

- Melt margarine in large frypan over low heat. Stir in garlic powder and sesame seed. Add Croutettes croutons, stirring until well coated. Cook, stirring frequently, until croutons are crisp and golden. Remove from heat. Set aside.

- In large salad bowl, toss salad greens with onion rings. Chill.

- For dressing, combine salt, pepper, dry mustard, vinegar and honey in small mixing bowl. Add oil slowly while beating with rotary beater or electric mixer. Chill.

- Just before serving, combine salad greens, tomato wedges, dressing and crisp croutons. Toss lightly.

Yield:    8 to 10 servings

# crisp croutons for salads or soups

**1/4 cup regular margarine or butter**
**2 cups Croutettes herb seasoned croutons**

- Melt margarine in large frypan over low heat. Add Croutettes croutons, stirring until well coated. Cook, stirring frequently, until croutons are crisped and lightly browned. Remove from heat.
- Toss croutons with salad greens or sprinkle over salad just before serving. Or serve generous spoonfuls atop soup.

Yield:   2 cups

**VARIATIONS:**

Any of the following may be stirred into melted margarine before adding Croutettes croutons:

**1/4 teaspoon garlic salt**
**1/4 teaspoon onion salt**
**2 tablespoons lemon juice**
**1 tablespoon Worcestershire sauce**
**2 drops liquid pepper sauce**

Any of the following may be tossed with the crisp golden croutons:

**2 teaspoons dill weed**
**2 tablespoons grated parmesan cheese**
**2 tablespoons dried parsley flakes**

# cheesed potato crisps

**3 tablespoons regular margarine or butter, melted**
**5 medium-size baking potatoes, pared**
**Salt**
**1-1/2 cups shredded American cheese**
**2 cups Corn Flakes cereal, crushed to measure 1 cup**
**Paprika**

- Brush melted margarine over bottom of 15-1/2 x 10-1/2 x 1-inch baking pan. Cut potatoes lengthwise into slices, about 1/4 inch thick. Arrange slices in single layer in pan, turning once to coat both sides with margarine.

- Sprinkle potatoes with salt, then with cheese. Top with crushed cereal. Sprinkle with paprika.

- Bake in oven at 375° F. about 25 minutes or until tender.

Yield:  6 servings

# potato-onion escallop

    5 tablespoons regular margarine or butter
  1/2 cup Corn Flake Crumbs
1-1/2 cups thinly sliced onions
4-1/2 cups thinly sliced, pared potatoes
    2 teaspoons salt
    3 tablespoons regular all-purpose flour
  1/4 teaspoon pepper
  1/4 teaspoon paprika
1-3/4 cups milk

- Melt 2 tablespoons of the margarine. Combine with Corn Flake Crumbs. Set aside for topping.

- Place onions and potatoes in medium-size saucepan. Cover with water. Add 1 teaspoon of the salt. Bring to boil. Boil, uncovered, for 5 minutes. Remove from heat. Drain.

- Melt the remaining 3 tablespoons margarine in small saucepan over low heat. Stir in flour, the remaining 1 teaspoon salt, the pepper and paprika. Add milk gradually, stirring until smooth. Increase heat to medium and cook until bubbly and thickened, stirring constantly. Remove from heat.

- Arrange one-third of the potatoes and onions in greased 10 x 6 x 2-inch (1-1/2-quart) glass baking dish. Top with one-third of the sauce. Repeat twice, ending with sauce. Sprinkle Crumbs mixture evenly over potato mixture. Bake in oven at 400° F. about 35 minutes or until potatoes are tender.

Yield:  6 to 8 servings

# green bean and onion salad

1/4 cup regular margarine or butter

1/2 teaspoon garlic salt

1-1/2 cups Croutettes herb seasoned croutons

2 packages (10 oz. each) frozen cut green beans,
cooked and drained

1 cup (4 oz.) thin strips Swiss cheese

1/2 teaspoon salt

Dash pepper

1/2 teaspoon basil leaves

1/2 teaspoon dry mustard

3 tablespoons vinegar

1 tablespoon honey

1/3 cup vegetable oil

Red onion rings

● Melt margarine in medium-size frypan over low heat. Stir in garlic salt. Add Croutettes croutons, stirring until well coated. Cook, stirring frequently, until croutons are crisp and golden. Remove from heat. Set aside.

● Combine beans and cheese in medium-size mixing bowl. Chill.

● To make dressing, measure salt, pepper, basil leaves, dry mustard, vinegar and honey into small mixing bowl. Add oil gradually, beating constantly. Chill.

● Just before serving, combine bean mixture, dressing and croutons, tossing lightly. Place 3/4-cup portions on lettuce leaves or in chilled individual dishes. Garnish with red onion rings.

Yield: 8 servings

# corn stuffing

1/2 cup regular margarine or butter

1-1/2 cups water or stock

1 can (12 oz.) whole kernel corn with sweet peppers, undrained

1 package (7 oz., 7 cups) Croutettes herb seasoned croutons

- Combine margarine, water and corn in large saucepan. Cook over medium heat, stirring occasionally, until mixture begins to boil. Remove from heat.

- Add Croutettes croutons all at one time, tossing lightly until croutons are evenly and thoroughly moistened. Cover pan tightly and let stand about 5 minutes. Serve immediately with suitable gravy or sauce, if desired.

Yield: 6 servings

# Hawaiian stuffing

1 can (20 oz.) pineapple chunks in pineapple juice

Water

1/2 cup regular margarine or butter

3 tablespoons firmly packed brown sugar

1 package (7 oz., 7 cups) Croutettes herb seasoned croutons

1/4 cup coarsely chopped nuts

1/4 cup seedless raisins

- Drain pineapple, reserving juice. Set pineapple aside. Add enough water to juice to measure 2 cups liquid. Combine margarine, sugar and the 2 cups liquid in large saucepan. Cook over medium heat, stirring occasionally, until mixture begins to boil. Remove from heat.

- Add Croutettes croutons all at one time, tossing lightly until croutons are evenly and thoroughly moistened. Add pineapple, nuts and raisins, mixing lightly. Spoon into greased 13-1/2 x 9 x 2-inch (3-quart) glass baking dish, pressing lightly.

- Bake in oven at 350° F. about 25 minutes or until thoroughly heated. Serve immediately as an accompaniment for ham, pork or poultry.

Yield: 8 servings

# grits casserole

3 tablespoons regular margarine or butter, melted
3/4 cup Corn Flake Crumbs
2 eggs
1/4 cup milk
4 cups water
1/2 teaspoon salt
1 cup quick-cooking grits
2 cups shredded American cheese
1/2 lb. bacon, fried crisp, crumbled

- Combine melted margarine with Corn Flake Crumbs. Set aside for topping.

- In small mixing bowl, beat eggs slightly. Stir in milk. Set aside.

- Measure water and salt into large saucepan. Bring to boil. Stir in grits. Cook over medium heat, stirring constantly, about 5 minutes. Remove from heat.

- Add cheese, stirring until melted. Stir in bacon and egg mixture. Spread in well-greased 12 x 7-1/2 x 2-inch (2-quart) glass baking dish. Sprinkle Crumbs mixture evenly over top.

- Bake in oven at 300° F. about 45 minutes or until thoroughly heated. Remove from oven. Let stand 5 to 10 minutes before serving.

Yield:  6 servings

# broccoli casserole

2 cups Croutettes herb seasoned croutons
3 tablespoons regular margarine or butter, melted
2 packages (10 oz. each) frozen chopped broccoli
1 cup shredded American cheese
1 can (10-3/4 oz.) condensed cream of mushroom soup

- Toss Croutettes croutons with melted margarine. Set aside for topping.

- Prepare broccoli according to package directions, cooking until almost tender. Remove from heat. Drain. Set aside.

- Combine cheese and soup in large saucepan. Cook over medium heat until cheese is melted, stirring frequently. Stir in broccoli. Pour into 10 x 6 x 2-inch (1-1/2-quart) glass baking dish. Top with croutons.

- Bake in oven at 350° F. about 20 minutes or until thoroughly heated and bubbly.

Yield:   6 servings

# crunchy bran topping

**2 tablespoons regular margarine or butter**
**1 cup All-Bran cereal or Bran Buds cereal**

- Melt margarine in small frypan over low heat. Stir in All-Bran cereal. Cook, stirring constantly, 2 to 3 minutes or until cereal is crisped and lightly browned.

- Sprinkle over soups, salads or creamed vegetables. Or omit cooking step and sprinkle over casseroles before baking.

Yield:   1 cup

**VARIATIONS:**

Any of the following may be tossed with the crisped cereal:

**1/4 teaspoon garlic salt**
**1 tablespoon grated parmesan cheese**
**1/2 teaspoon Italian seasoning**

# wilted lettuce salad

**2 tablespoons regular margarine or butter**
**3/4 teaspoon paprika**
**1/4 teaspoon garlic salt**
   **1 tablespoon sesame seed**
   **1 cup All-Bran cereal or Bran Buds cereal**
   **2 tablespoons grated parmesan cheese**
   **6 slices bacon**
   **2 quarts iceberg or leaf lettuce, torn into bite-size pieces**
     **(about 2 medium-size heads)**
   **1 large tomato, chopped**
**1/4 cup sliced green onions**
**1/2 teaspoon oregano leaves**
**1/4 teaspoon pepper**
**1/4 cup vinegar**
   **2 teaspoons sugar**

- Melt margarine in medium-size frypan over low heat. Stir in paprika, garlic salt and sesame seed. Add All-Bran cereal, stirring until well coated. Cook, stirring constantly, 2 to 3 minutes or until cereal is crisped and lightly browned. Remove from heat. Add parmesan cheese, tossing lightly. Set aside.

- Fry bacon until crisp. Drain, reserving 2 tablespoons drippings. Crumble bacon into small pieces. Set aside.

- In large mixing bowl, toss lettuce with tomato, green onions, oregano and pepper. Set aside.

- Combine reserved bacon drippings, vinegar and sugar in small saucepan. Bring to boil. Pour over lettuce. Cover bowl about 1 minute. Portion salad into individual salad bowls. Sprinkle bacon and cereal mixture over each portion. Serve immediately.

Yield: 6 servings

# festive corn custard

        **3 eggs, slightly beaten**
  **1-1/2 cups milk**
    **1/2 teaspoon salt**
      **1 teaspoon sugar**
    **1/4 cup finely chopped onion**
  **1-1/2 cups Croutettes herb seasoned croutons**
        **1 can (12 oz.) whole kernel corn with sweet peppers, drained**
    **1/4 cup sliced, pitted ripe olives**

- Combine all ingredients in large mixing bowl. Pour into well-greased 10 x 6 x 2-inch (1-1/2-quart) glass baking dish.
- Bake in oven at 350° F. about 55 minutes or until knife inserted near center comes out clean. Do not overbake. Cut into 6 pieces and serve immediately.

Yield:   6 servings

⩗    See page 189 for microwave directions.


# quick herbed tomatoes

        **2 tablespoons regular margarine or butter**
  **1/4 cup finely chopped onion**
      **2 cans (16 oz. each) whole peeled tomatoes, undrained**
    **1 tablespoon firmly packed brown sugar**
    **3/4 teaspoon salt**
  **1-1/2 cups Croutettes herb seasoned croutons**

- Melt margarine in large saucepan over low heat. Add onion. Cook, stirring frequently, until onion is softened but not browned.
- Stir in tomatoes, sugar and salt, cutting tomatoes into quarters with a spoon. Cook about 10 minutes longer or until thoroughly heated, stirring occasionally.
- Serve in individual vegetable dishes. Sprinkle Croutettes croutons over top.

Yield:   8 servings

# savory bran-rice pilaf

1/2 cup uncooked long grain white rice

1 chicken bouillon cube

6 tablespoons regular margarine or butter

1/4 cup chopped onion

1/2 cup chopped celery

1 jar (2-1/2 oz.) sliced mushrooms, drained

1/4 cup sliced water chestnuts

1 cup All-Bran cereal or Bran Buds cereal

1/4 teaspoon ground sage

1/2 teaspoon basil leaves

1/8 teaspoon pepper

1/2 cup water

- Cook rice according to package directions except omit salt and add bouillon cube.

- Melt 2 tablespoons of the margarine in large frypan. Stir in onion, celery, mushrooms and water chestnuts. Cook over medium heat, stirring occasionally, about 10 minutes or until celery is almost tender. Add the remaining 4 tablespoons margarine. Stir until melted.

- Gently stir in cooked rice, All-Bran cereal, sage, basil leaves, pepper and water. Cover and cook over very low heat about 15 minutes. Serve immediately.

Yield:   6 servings

# stuffing squares

1 egg

1 can (10-3/4 oz.) condensed cream of mushroom soup

1 cup water

1 package (7 oz., 7 cups) Croutettes herb seasoned croutons

- In large mixing bowl, beat egg until foamy. Add soup and water, stirring until well combined. Add Croutettes croutons all at one time, tossing lightly until croutons are evenly and thoroughly moistened. Spoon into well-greased 8 x 8 x 2-inch baking pan, pressing lightly.

- Bake in oven at 375° F. about 30 minutes or until set. Cut into squares.

Yield:   9 servings

**VARIATIONS:**

Add any of the following to soup mixture:

**1/3 cup chopped mushrooms**

**1/2 cup toasted slivered almonds**

**1/4 cup snipped fresh parsley and 2 tablespoons chopped pimiento**

  See page 190 for microwave directions.

# crunchy apple rings

**1/2 cup regular all-purpose flour**

**1/2 teaspoon baking powder**

**1/4 teaspoon salt**

**1/2 teaspoon ground cinnamon**

**1/8 teaspoon ground nutmeg**

**1 egg, separated**

**2 tablespoons sugar**

**1/3 cup milk**

**2 apples, cored and sliced into thin rings**

**4 cups Corn Flakes cereal, crushed to measure 1-3/4 cups**

**Vegetable oil or shortening (for frying)**

**Confectioners' sugar**

- Stir together flour, baking powder, salt, cinnamon and nutmeg. Set aside.

- In small mixing bowl, beat egg white until foamy. Add sugar. Beat until stiff but not dry. Set aside. In a second small mixing bowl, beat egg yolk with milk. Stir in flour mixture. Fold in beaten egg white.

- Dip apple rings in batter. Coat with crushed cereal. Fry in 1/4 inch of oil at 385° F., turning once, about 1 minute on each side. Drain on absorbent paper. Dust with confectioners' sugar. Serve plain or with maple syrup.

Yield:   6 to 8 servings

# crunchy Rice Krispies topping

**1 tablespoon regular margarine or butter**
**1 cup Rice Krispies cereal**

- Melt margarine in small frypan over low heat. Remove from heat. Add Rice Krispies cereal, stirring until well coated.
- Spoon over top of vegetable or main dish casserole before baking. For use on soups or salads, cook cereal in frypan until crisped and lightly browned. Remove from heat. Sprinkle over hot soup or crisp green salad just before serving.

Yield:  1 cup

## VARIATIONS:

Any of the following may be stirred into melted margarine before adding cereal:

**1/8 teaspoon garlic salt**
**1/8 teaspoon onion salt**
**1/4 teaspoon chili powder**
**1/4 teaspoon curry powder**
**1/2 teaspoon paprika**
**1 teaspoon Worcestershire sauce**
**6 to 8 drops liquid pepper sauce**

Any of the following may be tossed with the crisped cereal:

**1 teaspoon dill weed**
**1 tablespoon dried parsley flakes**
**1 tablespoon grated parmesan cheese**

See page 190 for microwave directions.

# bran topped cauliflower escallop

**2 tablespoons regular margarine or butter, melted**
**1/4 teaspoon garlic salt**
**1/2 cup All-Bran cereal or Bran Buds cereal**
**4 cups sliced cauliflower (1 medium-size head)**
**1 chicken bouillon cube**
**3/4 cup hot water**
**1/4 cup regular margarine or butter**
**1/4 cup regular all-purpose flour**
**1/2 teaspoon salt**
**1/8 teaspoon white pepper**
**1 cup half-and-half**
**2 tablespoons chopped pimiento**
**1 cup sliced green onions**

- Combine the 2 tablespoons melted margarine with the garlic salt and All-Bran cereal. Set aside for topping.

- Cook cauliflower in small amount of water until almost tender, about 10 minutes. Drain well. Set aside.

- Dissolve bouillon cube in the 3/4 cup hot water. Set aside.

- Melt the 1/4 cup margarine in large saucepan over low heat. Stir in flour, salt and pepper. Add bouillon and half-and-half gradually, stirring until smooth. Increase heat to medium and cook until bubbly and thickened, stirring constantly. Remove from heat. Stir in pimiento, green onions and cauliflower. Spoon mixture into 10 x 6 x 2-inch (1-1/2-quart) glass baking dish. Sprinkle cereal mixture evenly over top.

- Bake in oven at 350° F. about 20 minutes or until thoroughly heated and bubbly.

Yield: 6 to 8 servings

**VARIATION:**

2 packages (10 oz. each) frozen cauliflower, cooked and drained, may be substituted for fresh cauliflower.

# carrots au gratin

    5 tablespoons regular margarine or butter
1/2 cup Corn Flake Crumbs
1/3 cup chopped onion
    3 tablespoons regular all-purpose flour
    1 teaspoon salt
1/8 teaspoon pepper
1-1/2 cups milk
    1 cup shredded American cheese
    4 cups sliced carrots, cooked and drained (about 1-1/2 lbs.)
    1 tablespoon dried parsley flakes

● Melt 2 tablespoons of the margarine. Combine with Corn Flake Crumbs. Set aside for topping.

● Melt the remaining 3 tablespoons margarine in large saucepan over low heat. Add onion. Cook, stirring frequently, until onion is softened but not browned. Stir in flour, salt and pepper. Add milk gradually, stirring until smooth. Increase heat to medium and cook until bubbly and thickened, stirring constantly. Add cheese, stirring until melted. Remove from heat. Stir in carrots and parsley flakes. Spread mixture in greased 10 x 6 x 2-inch (1-1/2-quart) glass baking dish. Sprinkle Crumbs mixture evenly over top.

● Bake in oven at 350° F. about 20 minutes or until thoroughly heated and bubbly. Remove from oven. Let stand about 5 minutes before serving.

Yield:   8 servings

   See page 191 for microwave directions.


# fettuccini

1/2 cup Corn Flake Crumbs
    1 cup grated parmesan cheese
    1 package (12 oz.) broad egg noodles
1/2 cup regular margarine or butter, softened
    2 tablespoons snipped fresh parsley

- Stir together Corn Flake Crumbs and cheese. Set aside.

- Cook noodles according to package directions. Drain. Do not rinse. In large mixing bowl, gently toss hot noodles with margarine. Add parsley and Crumbs mixture, tossing until combined. Serve immediately.

Yield:  6 to 8 servings

# herbed zucchini bake

**2-1/4 cups Croutettes herb seasoned croutons**
**2 tablespoons regular margarine or butter, melted**
**4 medium-size zucchini squash, cubed**
**1/4 cup regular margarine or butter**
**3/4 cup grated carrots**
**1/2 cup chopped onions**
**1 can (10-3/4 oz.) condensed cream of chicken soup**
**1/2 cup dairy sour cream**
**1 tablespoon chopped pimiento**
**1 teaspoon salt**
**1/4 teaspoon pepper**

- Toss 3/4 cup of the Croutettes croutons with the 2 tablespoons melted margarine. Set aside for topping.

- In large saucepan, cook zucchini squash in lightly salted water until tender, about 5 minutes. Drain.

- Melt the 1/4 cup margarine in large saucepan. Add carrots and onions. Cook over low heat until tender. Remove from heat. Add the remaining 1-1/2 cups croutons, the soup, sour cream, pimiento, salt and pepper. Mix thoroughly. Stir in cooked squash. Spread in ungreased 10 x 6 x 2-inch (1-1/2-quart) glass baking dish. Top with reserved croutons.

- Bake in oven at 350° F. about 35 minutes or until thoroughly heated and bubbly.

Yield:   8 servings

See page 192 for microwave directions.

# crispy potato balls

1 egg, separated
1/2 teaspoon dried parsley flakes
1-1/2 cups seasoned, very stiff mashed potatoes
2/3 cup Corn Flake Crumbs
2 tablespoons regular margarine or butter, melted

- Combine egg yolk and parsley flakes in small mixing bowl. Add potatoes. Mix until thoroughly combined. Set aside.

- In small shallow dish, beat egg white until foamy. Set aside.

- Portion potato mixture by level measuring-tablespoon. Shape into balls. Dip balls in egg white. Coat evenly with Corn Flake Crumbs. Place in well-greased or foil-lined shallow baking pan. Do not crowd. Drizzle with melted margarine.

- Bake in oven at 450° F. about 10 minutes or until lightly browned.

Yield:   6 servings, about 4 balls each

NOTE:   For best results, mashed potatoes should be stiff enough so that mixture appears crumbly and slightly dry.

## VARIATIONS:

Any of the following may be added with the mashed potatoes in step 1:

1/3 cup whole kernel corn, cooked and drained
1/3 cup crumbled fried bacon
1/3 cup shredded sharp cheddar cheese
1/4 cup grated parmesan cheese
1/4 cup chopped green onions (omit parsley)

# stuffin' muffins

**1 package (7 oz., 7 cups) Croutettes herb seasoned croutons**
**1/2 cup regular margarine or butter, melted**
**1-1/2 cups hot water or stock**

- In large mixing bowl, toss Croutettes croutons with melted margarine. Stir lightly while adding hot water or stock.

- Divide prepared stuffing into 12 portions, using approximately 1/2 cup for each portion. Shape into balls. Place in 12 greased 2-1/2-inch muffin-pan cups. Cover tightly with foil.

- Bake in oven at 350° F. about 30 minutes. Serve immediately with suitable gravy or sauce, if desired.

Yield:   6 servings, 2 muffins each

## VARIATIONS:

**Celery-Onion Stuffin' Muffins:**   Cook 1/2 cup finely chopped celery and 1/4 cup chopped onion in the margarine just until tender before tossing with the croutons.

**Fresh Mushroom Stuffin' Muffins:**   Cook 1 cup sliced fresh mushrooms in the margarine until lightly browned before tossing with the croutons.

# poultry stuffing

See *Croutettes Stuffing Guide* on page 117.

# MEATS

# MEATS

Meat has historically been the center of attention at mealtime. An excellent source of protein, meats can be combined with cereals, vegetables and dairy products to make exceptional main dishes from unusual sandwiches to hearty casseroles.

1. meatball stew, p. 92
2. schnitzel, p. 92
3. baked stuffed pork chops, p. 88
4. Mexican stuffed peppers, p. 91
5. busy-day meatloaf, p. 95

6. good and spicy meatballs, p. 87
7. crunchy ham and cheese sandwiches, p. 93
8. meat 'n tater pie, p. 98
9. Cornish beef pasties, p. 103

# good and spicy meatballs

          1 egg
          1 cup Rice Krispies cereal
    1/4 cup finely chopped onion
    2/3 cup instant nonfat dry milk (in dry form)
       2 tablespoons catsup
       1 teaspoon salt
    1/8 teaspoon pepper
       1 lb. ground beef

              *         *         *         *         *

       1 can (15 oz.) tomato sauce
    1/2 cup catsup
    1/2 cup water
    1/4 cup firmly packed brown sugar
    1/4 cup finely chopped onion
    1/4 cup pickle relish
       2 tablespoons Worcestershire sauce
       1 tablespoon vinegar
    1/4 teaspoon pepper

- In large mixing bowl, beat egg slightly. Add next 6 ingredients. Mix well. Add ground beef. Mix until combined. Portion meat mixture using level measuring-tablespoon. Shape into meatballs. Place in single layer in greased or foil-lined shallow baking pan.

- Bake in oven at 400° F. about 12 minutes or until well browned.

- For sauce, measure remaining ingredients into large saucepan. Stir to combine. Cover. Cook over low heat about 15 minutes, stirring frequently. Add meatballs to sauce. Cook over low heat about 10 minutes longer. Serve over rice, if desired.

Yield:   6 servings

# beef 'n bean skillet

1-1/2 cups Product 19 multivitamin and iron supplement cereal,
    crushed to measure 3/4 cup
1/4 cup chopped onion
1 teaspoon salt
1/8 teaspoon pepper
1 tablespoon Worcestershire sauce
1/3 cup milk
1 lb. ground beef
1 can (10-3/4 oz.) condensed tomato soup
1 can (1 lb.) pork and beans
1/2 teaspoon chili powder
1/2 cup shredded American cheese

- Measure first 6 ingredients into large mixing bowl. Beat well. Add ground beef. Mix until combined. Shape into 6 patties.

- Brown patties on both sides in large frypan over medium heat. Drain off excess drippings. Add soup, pork and beans and chili powder. Stir gently to combine. Cover. Cook over low heat about 30 minutes or until patties are thoroughly cooked, stirring carefully once or twice. Remove cover. Sprinkle with cheese. Cook 1 to 2 minutes longer or until cheese melts. Serve in individual bowls.

Yield:   6 servings


# baked stuffed pork chops

1/4 cup regular margarine or butter
1/2 cup finely chopped onions
2 tablespoons finely chopped celery
1/2 cup water or stock
1/2 package (3-1/2 cups) Croutettes herb seasoned croutons
4 pork chops, 1-1/2 inches thick, cut with pockets
Salt
Pepper

- Melt margarine in medium-size saucepan over low heat. Add onions and celery. Cook, stirring frequently, until softened but not browned. Add water. Bring to boil. Remove from heat. Add Croutettes croutons all at one time, tossing lightly until croutons are evenly and thoroughly moistened.

- If necessary, extend pocket in each pork chop to bone. Fill with croutons mixture. Fasten edges with wooden picks. Place stuffed chops, flat side down, in shallow baking pan. Do not crowd. Sprinkle with salt and pepper. Cover pan tightly with foil.

- Bake in oven at 350° F. about 55 minutes. Uncover and bake about 30 minutes longer or until chops are browned and tender.

Yield:   4 servings

# Spanish rice pie

1-1/2 cups Product 19 multivitamin and iron supplement cereal, crushed to measure 3/4 cup

1/2 cup milk

1/4 cup chopped onion

1 teaspoon salt

1 lb. ground beef

1 can (15 oz.) tomato sauce

1 cup uncooked instant rice

2 tablespoons finely chopped green pepper

1/4 teaspoon chili powder

1/2 cup shredded American cheese

- Measure crushed Product 19 supplement cereal, milk, onion and salt into large mixing bowl. Stir to combine. Add ground beef. Mix until combined. Press evenly around sides and in bottom of 9-inch pie pan to form meat pie shell. Set aside.

- In medium-size mixing bowl, stir together tomato sauce, uncooked instant rice, green pepper and chili powder. Spoon into meat shell, spreading evenly.

- Bake in oven at 350° F. about 30 minutes or until meat pulls away from side of pan. Remove from oven. Sprinkle with cheese. Return to oven and bake about 3 minutes longer or until cheese melts. Cut into wedges to serve.

Yield:   6 servings

# saucy stroganoff

1 beef bouillon cube
3/4 cup boiling water
1 egg
3 tablespoons catsup
1 tablespoon prepared mustard
1/4 cup finely chopped onion
1/4 teaspoon liquid pepper sauce
1 teaspoon salt
1/2 cup Corn Flake Crumbs
1-1/2 lbs. ground beef

       *       *       *       *       *

1/2 cup water
1 beef bouillon cube
1 can (10-3/4 oz.) condensed cream of mushroom soup
1 carton (8 oz., 1 cup) dairy sour cream
1 can (3 oz.) sliced mushrooms, drained
2 teaspoons Worcestershire sauce
1/4 teaspoon instant minced garlic
3 teaspoons dried parsley flakes
Hot cooked noodles

- In large mixing bowl, dissolve 1 bouillon cube in the 3/4 cup water. Add next 7 ingredients. Beat well. Add ground beef. Mix until combined. Portion meat mixture using level measuring-tablespoon. Shape into meatballs. Place in single layer in greased or foil-lined shallow baking pan.

- Bake in oven at 400° F. about 15 minutes or until well browned.

- For sauce, heat the 1/2 cup water and the remaining bouillon cube in medium-size saucepan over low heat until cube is dissolved. Stir in soup, sour cream, mushrooms, Worcestershire sauce, garlic and 2 teaspoons of the parsley flakes. Cook, stirring frequently, until sauce is thoroughly heated.

- Serve meatballs on hot cooked noodles. Pour sauce over meatballs. Sprinkle with remaining 1 teaspoon parsley flakes.

Yield:  6 servings

# Mexican stuffed peppers

6 large green peppers
1 lb. ground beef
1 medium-size onion, sliced
2 cups Rice Krispies cereal
1/8 teaspoon instant minced garlic
2 teaspoons chili powder
1 teaspoon salt
1/8 teaspoon pepper
1 teaspoon sugar
1/2 cup sliced, pitted ripe olives
1 can (6 oz.) tomato paste
1 can (16 oz.) whole peeled tomatoes, drained
1/2 cup shredded sharp cheddar cheese

- Wash peppers. Cut off tops and remove seedy portions. Precook in large amount of boiling water about 5 minutes. Drain well. Place peppers, cut side up, in greased shallow baking pan. Set aside.

- In large frypan, cook ground beef and onion until meat is browned, stirring frequently. Drain off excess drippings. Add remaining ingredients except cheese. Stir to combine, cutting tomatoes into pieces with spoon. Remove from heat. Spoon into peppers, dividing evenly.

- Bake in oven at 350° F. about 25 minutes or until filling is thoroughly heated. Remove from oven. Sprinkle tops with cheese. Return to oven. Bake about 5 minutes longer or until cheese melts.

Yield:  6 servings

## VARIATIONS:

**Corny Stuffed Peppers:**  2 cups Corn Flakes cereal may be substituted for the Rice Krispies cereal.

**Mexican Sloppy Joes:**  Omit green peppers and cheese. After mixing all ingredients together, cover frypan. Cook mixture over very low heat about 15 minutes. Serve on toasted hamburger buns. Yield:  6 to 8 servings

See page 186 for microwave directions.

91

# meatball stew

2 cups Corn Flakes cereal, crushed to measure 1 cup
1 egg
1 can (10-1/2 oz., 1-1/4 cups) condensed beef broth soup
1/2 teaspoon salt
1/8 teaspoon pepper
1 lb. ground beef
2 tablespoons vegetable oil
1 can (10-3/4 oz.) condensed tomato soup
1/2 cup water
2 cups frozen sliced carrots
1 medium-size onion, sliced, separated into rings
1 can (1 lb.) whole white potatoes, drained
1/4 teaspoon ground thyme

- Measure crushed Corn Flakes cereal, egg, 1/4 cup of the broth, the salt and pepper into large mixing bowl. Beat well. Add ground beef. Mix until combined. Shape into 18 meatballs.

- Brown meatballs in oil in large frypan over medium heat. Drain off excess drippings. Stir in the remaining 1 cup broth, the tomato soup, water, carrots, onion rings, potatoes and thyme. Cover. Cook over medium heat about 25 minutes or until meatballs are thoroughly cooked.

Yield:   6 servings

# schnitzel

2 cups Rice Krispies cereal, crushed to fine crumbs
1 egg
3 tablespoons water
1/4 cup regular all-purpose flour
1/2 teaspoon salt
1/4 teaspoon pepper
1 lb. pork cutlets, 1/4 to 1/2 inch thick
1/2 cup regular margarine or butter
3 tablespoons lemon juice
1 tablespoon snipped fresh parsley

- Place crushed Rice Krispies cereal in shallow dish or pan. Set aside.

- In a second shallow dish or pan, beat egg and water until foamy.

- In a third shallow dish or pan, stir together flour, salt and pepper. Dip cutlets in flour mixture. Then dip in egg mixture. Coat with crushed cereal.

- Melt 1/4 cup of the margarine in large frypan over low heat. Increase heat to medium. Brown cutlets in melted margarine on both sides. Reduce heat to low. Cover. Cook about 20 minutes or until cutlets are tender.

- In small saucepan, melt the remaining 1/4 cup margarine. Bring to boil. Immediately remove from heat. Stir in lemon juice and parsley. Pour over cutlets. Garnish each serving with lemon slice topped with anchovy and a few capers, if desired.

Yield:   4 servings

# crunchy ham and cheese sandwiches

**3 cups Rice Krispies cereal, crushed to measure 1-1/2 cups**
**2 eggs**
**1/2 cup milk**
**1/4 teaspoon salt**
**4 slices cheese**
**4 thin slices cooked ham**
**8 slices day-old bread**
**3 tablespoons regular margarine or butter, melted**

- Place crushed Rice Krispies cereal in shallow dish or pan. Set aside.

- In a second shallow dish or pan, beat eggs, milk and salt until foamy. Set aside.

- Make 4 sandwiches using 1 slice cheese, 1 slice ham and 2 slices bread for each. Dip sandwiches quickly in egg mixture, turning once. Coat with crushed cereal. Place in single layer on well-greased baking sheet. Drizzle with melted margarine.

- Bake in oven at 450° F. about 15 minutes or until crisp and golden brown.

Yield:   4 servings

# apple-glazed ham loaf

1 jar (10 oz.) apple jelly

1/4 cup firmly packed brown sugar

3 tablespoons lemon juice

1/2 teaspoon dry mustard

\*         \*         \*         \*         \*

2 eggs

3/4 cup Corn Flake Crumbs

1/4 cup firmly packed brown sugar

3/4 cup milk

1/3 cup finely chopped onion

1/2 teaspoon salt (optional)

1/8 teaspoon pepper

1-1/2 teaspoons dry mustard

1 lb. ground cooked ham

1 lb. ground pork

- For glaze, stir together jelly, the 1/4 cup sugar, the lemon juice and the 1/2 teaspoon dry mustard in small saucepan. Cook over low heat, stirring frequently, until jelly melts. Bring to boil. Boil 1 minute, stirring constantly. Remove from heat. Cool to room temperature.

- In large mixing bowl, beat eggs slightly. Add Corn Flake Crumbs, the remaining 1/4 cup sugar, the milk, onion, salt, pepper and the remaining 1-1/2 teaspoons dry mustard. Beat well. Add ham and pork. Mix until combined. Shape into loaf. Place in greased or foil-lined shallow baking pan.

- Bake in oven at 350° F. about 1 hour and 15 minutes or until well browned. Brush loaf with glaze several times during last 30 minutes of baking. Serve with remaining glaze.

Yield:   10 to 12 servings

# busy-day meatloaf

        1 cup Croutettes herb seasoned croutons
    1/2 cup milk
        1 egg
        2 teaspoons Worcestershire sauce
    1/4 cup finely chopped onion
        1 teaspoon salt
        1 lb. ground beef
            Catsup or chili sauce

- Combine Croutettes croutons and milk in large mixing bowl. Let stand about 5 minutes or until croutons are softened. Add egg, Worcestershire sauce, onion and salt. Beat well. Add ground beef. Mix until combined.

- Shape into loaf. Place in greased or foil-lined shallow baking pan. Score loaf by making several diagonal grooves across top. Fill with catsup.

- Bake in oven at 350° F. about 45 minutes or until well browned.

Yield:  5 to 6 servings

See page 184 for microwave directions.


# zippy dipped franks

        10 wooden skewers, 4-1/2 inches long
        10 frankfurters
        1/2 cup catsup, mustard or mixture of catsup and mustard
        1/2 cup Corn Flake Crumbs

- Insert skewers lengthwise into frankfurters, leaving about 2 inches for handles. Dip frankfurters in catsup. Coat with Corn Flake Crumbs. Place in greased or foil-lined shallow baking pan.

- Bake in oven at 400° F. about 12 minutes or until crisped and thoroughly heated. Serve with additional catsup or mustard, if desired.

Yield:  5 servings, 2 frankfurters each

# sausage bran corncake

1-1/4 cups regular all-purpose flour

  3 teaspoons baking powder

  1 teaspoon salt

  2 tablespoons sugar

  1 can (8-3/4 oz.) whole kernel corn, drained, reserving liquid
    Milk

  1/4 cup vegetable oil

  2 eggs

  1 cup All-Bran cereal or Bran Buds cereal

 24 fully cooked breakfast sausage links


● Stir together flour, baking powder, salt and sugar. Set aside.

● To reserved corn liquid, add milk to measure 1 cup. Place milk mixture, corn, oil, eggs and All-Bran cereal in large mixing bowl. Mix well. Add flour mixture, mixing until well combined. Spread batter evenly in well-greased 15-1/2 x 10-1/2 x 1-inch baking pan. Arrange sausage links over batter in 2 uniform rows.

● Bake in oven at 400° F. about 25 minutes or until lightly browned. Serve warm with maple syrup, applesauce or *Cheese Sauce.*

Yield:  8 servings


**VARIATIONS:**

**Corny Corncake:**  1/2 cup Corn Flake Crumbs may be substituted for the All-Bran cereal.

**Western Corncake:**  Stir 1/4 cup finely chopped green pepper and 2 tablespoons finely chopped onion into batter. Serve with *Cheese Sauce.*

# cheese sauce

2 tablespoons regular margarine or butter

2 tablespoons regular all-purpose flour

1/4 teaspoon dry mustard

1-1/3 cups milk

2 cups shredded American cheese

1/4 teaspoon Worcestershire sauce

1 tablespoon chopped chives

● Melt margarine in small saucepan over low heat. Stir in flour and mustard. Add milk gradually, stirring until smooth. Increase heat to medium and cook until bubbly and thickened, stirring constantly.

● Add cheese and Worcestershire sauce. Stir until cheese is melted. Sprinkle with chives.

Yield: 2 cups

# chili

1 lb. ground beef

1 large onion, sliced

1/2 cup chopped green pepper

1 cup All-Bran cereal or Bran Buds cereal

1 can (16 oz.) red kidney beans, undrained

1 can (16 oz.) whole peeled tomatoes, undrained

1 can (8 oz.) tomato sauce

1/2 cup water

1 tablespoon chili powder

1/8 teaspoon garlic powder

1 teaspoon salt

1-1/2 teaspoons sugar

1 bay leaf

● In large saucepan, cook ground beef, onion and green pepper until meat is browned. Stir in remaining ingredients, cutting tomatoes into pieces with spoon. Cover. Cook over low heat about 1 hour. Stir occasionally.

Yield: 6 servings

# meat 'n tater pie

1 cup Corn Flake Crumbs

1 teaspoon salt

1/4 teaspoon pepper

1 tablespoon prepared mustard

1/3 cup milk

1 lb. ground beef

2 eggs

2 cups seasoned, stiff mashed potatoes

1/4 cup chopped onion

2 teaspoons dried parsley flakes

2 tablespoons regular margarine or butter, melted

1/2 cup shredded American cheese

Paprika

- Measure 1/2 cup of the Corn Flake Crumbs, the salt, pepper, mustard and milk into large mixing bowl. Beat well. Add ground beef. Mix until combined. Spread evenly in 9 x 9 x 2-inch baking pan. Set aside.

- In small mixing bowl, beat eggs slightly. Add potatoes, onion and parsley flakes. Stir until combined. Spread potato mixture evenly over meat mixture.

- Bake in oven at 350° F. about 35 minutes. While pie is baking, combine the remaining 1/2 cup Corn Flake Crumbs with melted margarine. Set aside.

- Remove pie from oven. Sprinkle cheese evenly over potato mixture. Top with Crumbs mixture. Bake about 10 minutes longer or until cheese melts. Sprinkle with paprika.

Yield:   6 servings

**VARIATION:**

*Meat 'n Tater Pie* may also be made in 9-inch pie pan. Gently press meat mixture evenly around sides and in bottom of pan to form meat pie shell. Fill with potato mixture. Place on baking sheet and bake as directed in step 3.

See page 187 for microwave directions.

98

# tamale pie

2 tablespoons shortening

1 medium-size onion, chopped

1 medium-size green pepper, chopped

1 lb. ground beef

1 can (8 oz.) stewed tomatoes

1 can (8 oz.) tomato sauce

1 package (1-3/4 oz.) seasoning mix for chili

1 tablespoon sugar

     *       *       *       *       *

3/4 cup Corn Flake Crumbs

3/4 cup regular all-purpose flour

2 teaspoons baking powder

3/4 teaspoon salt

2 teaspoons sugar

1 egg

1/2 cup milk

1/4 cup chopped ripe olives

3 tablespoons regular margarine or butter, softened

- Melt shortening in large frypan. Add onion, green pepper and ground beef. Cook until meat is browned and vegetables are tender. Drain off fat.

- Add tomatoes, tomato sauce, seasoning mix and the 1 tablespoon sugar. Mix well. Pour into greased 2-quart casserole. Set aside.

- Stir together Corn Flake Crumbs, flour, baking powder, salt and the 2 teaspoons sugar. Set aside.

- In large mixing bowl, combine egg, milk, olives and margarine. Beat well. Add flour mixture, mixing until well combined. Spread batter evenly over meat mixture.

- Bake in oven at 350° F. about 45 minutes or until topping is lightly browned and wooden pick inserted near center comes out clean.

Yield: 6 servings

# quick savory meatloaf

1 egg
3/4 cup milk
1 teaspoon salt
1/8 teaspoon pepper
1 teaspoon dry mustard
1 tablespoon Worcestershire sauce
1/3 cup finely chopped onion
2 cups Rice Krispies cereal
1-1/2 lbs. ground beef

- In large mixing bowl, beat egg slightly. Stir in remaining ingredients except ground beef. Let stand about 5 minutes or until Rice Krispies cereal is softened. Beat well. Add ground beef. Mix until combined. Shape into loaf. Place in greased or foil-lined shallow baking pan.
- Bake in oven at 350° F. about 1 hour or until well browned. Serve with *Golden Mushroom Sauce* or *Horseradish Sauce.*

Yield:   8 servings

**VARIATION:**

**Savory Cheeseburgers:**   Shape mixture into 8 patties. Place in single layer in greased or foil-lined shallow baking pan. Bake in oven at 350° F. about 25 minutes. A few minutes before end of baking time, top each with cheese slice. Serve on toasted hamburger buns.   Yield:   8 servings

# golden mushroom sauce

1 can (10-3/4 oz.) condensed golden mushroom soup
1/4 cup red wine

- Heat soup in small saucepan over low heat, stirring frequently. Stir in wine. Continue cooking until mixture boils. Serve immediately.

Yield:   1-1/4 cups

# horseradish sauce

 1 carton (8 oz., 1 cup) dairy sour cream
1/4 cup prepared horseradish
 1 tablespoon chopped chives
1/2 teaspoon salt
 1 tablespoon milk

● Measure all ingredients into small mixing bowl. Stir to combine. Chill until serving time. Serve cold.

Yield:  1 cup


# veal scaloppini

 1 cup Corn Flake Crumbs
 1 teaspoon salt
1/8 teaspoon pepper
 2 lbs. boneless veal cutlets, 1/4 inch thick
 1 clove garlic, quartered
1/2 cup olive oil
 2 cups sliced fresh mushrooms
 1 can (10-1/2 oz., 1-1/4 cups) condensed beef broth soup
 1 tablespoon lemon juice

● Stir together Corn Flake Crumbs, salt and pepper. Set aside.

● Cut veal cutlets into pieces of similar size and shape. Sprinkle Crumbs mixture over cutlets. Pound with meat mallet. Repeat on other side of cutlets.

● In large frypan, cook garlic in olive oil over medium heat until browned. Add cutlets and fry until golden brown on both sides and thoroughly cooked. Place cutlets on heated platter.

● Add mushrooms to remaining oil in frypan. Cook until lightly browned. Stir in broth and lemon juice. Bring to boil. Pour over cutlets.

Yield:  6 to 8 servings

# ham croquettes

1/2 cup Corn Flake Crumbs

2 tablespoons finely chopped onion

2 eggs

1/3 cup catsup

1/2 teaspoon dry mustard

1-1/2 lbs. coarsely ground cooked ham

*     *     *     *     *

1 egg

2 tablespoons water

3/4 cup Corn Flake Crumbs

Vegetable oil or shortening (for frying)

- Measure first 5 ingredients into medium-size mixing bowl. Beat well. Add ham. Mix until combined. Shape into 16 croquettes. Set aside. In a shallow dish, beat remaining egg and water until foamy. Dip croquettes in egg mixture. Coat evenly with the 3/4 cup Corn Flake Crumbs.

- Fry in deep hot oil at 375° F. about 4 minutes or until golden brown. Drain on absorbent paper. Serve with *Parsley Mustard Sauce.*

Yield:   8 servings, 2 croquettes each

# parsley mustard sauce

2 tablespoons regular margarine or butter

2 tablespoons regular all-purpose flour

1/4 teaspoon salt

1 cup milk

1 teaspoon prepared mustard

2 tablespoons prepared horseradish

1 tablespoon finely snipped fresh parsley

- Melt margarine in small saucepan over low heat. Stir in flour and salt. Add milk gradually, stirring until smooth. Increase heat to medium and cook until bubbly and thickened, stirring constantly. Remove from heat. Stir in mustard, horseradish and parsley.  Yield:   1 cup

# Cornish beef pasties

        1 lb. beef round steak, cut into 1/4-inch cubes
1/2 cup finely cubed, peeled potatoes
1/2 cup finely cubed, peeled turnips
1/2 cup finely cubed carrots
1/2 cup finely chopped onions
        1 teaspoon salt
1/4 teaspoon pepper

            *           *           *           *           *

        1 package (11 oz.) pie crust mix
1/2 cup Corn Flake Crumbs
        7 tablespoons cold water

- In large mixing bowl, combine beef, potatoes, turnips, carrots, onions, salt and pepper. Set aside.

- Stir together pie crust mix and Corn Flake Crumbs. Add water, mixing with fork until dough holds together. Add 1 to 2 teaspoons additional water, if needed.

- Divide dough into 6 equal portions. On lightly floured surface, roll each portion to a 7-inch circle. Top each with 3/4 cup meat mixture. Moisten edge with water. Fold in half and press edges to seal, using tines of fork. Cut 2 or 3 slits in pasties for steam to escape. Place on ungreased baking sheet.

- Bake in oven at 400° F. about 45 minutes or until golden brown. Serve with gravy, if desired.

Yield:  6 servings

# cheesy potluck casserole

Use 1 cup cubed cooked ham in place of tuna in the recipe for *Cheesy Potluck Casserole* that appears on page 110.

FISH

# FISH

Be it fresh, frozen or canned, fish has become a popular entree year 'round. Its delicate flavor, ease of preparation and nutritional value have made fish of all varieties "a delicious catch" for our daily meals.

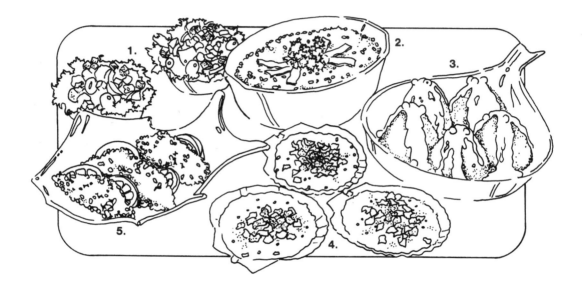

1. apple mélange salad, p. 112
2. cheesy potluck casserole, p. 110
3. corn-crisped salmon croquettes, p. 110
4. baked seafood salad, p. 113
5. baked fish fillets, p. 111

# quick 'n easy tuna loaf

2 cans (7 oz. each) solid pack white tuna, drained and flaked
2 eggs, slightly beaten
1/2 cup milk
1/2 teaspoon salt
1/8 teaspoon pepper
1 teaspoon lemon juice
2 tablespoons pickle relish
2 cups Special K cereal

- Combine all ingredients in medium-size mixing bowl. Mix well. Spread evenly in well-greased 9 x 5 x 3-inch loaf pan.
- Bake in oven at 350° F. about 20 minutes. Serve hot with *Egg Sauce*. Sprinkle with paprika or snipped fresh parsley, if desired.

Yield:  6 servings


# egg sauce

2 tablespoons regular margarine or butter
2 tablespoons regular all-purpose flour
1/8 teaspoon salt
1 cup milk
2 tablespoons lemon juice
1 hard-cooked egg, chopped

- Melt margarine in small saucepan over low heat. Stir in flour and salt. Add milk gradually, stirring until smooth.
- Increase heat to medium and cook until bubbly and thickened, stirring constantly. Just before serving, stir in lemon juice and egg.

Yield:  1-1/3 cups

# tangy topped salmon bake

1/3 cup dairy sour cream

1/2 cup milk

3 eggs, separated

2 cups Rice Krispies cereal

1 can (15-1/2 oz.) salmon, drained, skinned, boned and flaked

1/4 cup finely chopped onion

1/4 cup chopped celery

1 tablespoon dried parsley flakes

1 tablespoon lemon juice

1/2 teaspoon salt

1/8 teaspoon pepper

1 cup mayonnaise

1 tablespoon prepared mustard

- In large mixing bowl, stir together sour cream, milk and egg yolks. Add Rice Krispies cereal, stirring until combined. Let stand about 5 minutes. Beat well. Add salmon, onion, celery, 2 teaspoons of the parsley flakes, lemon juice, salt and pepper. Mix until combined. Set aside.

- Place 2 of the egg whites in small mixing bowl. Beat until stiff but not dry. Fold into salmon mixture. Spread in well-greased 10 x 6 x 2-inch (1-1/2-quart) glass baking dish.

- Bake in oven at 375° F. about 30 minutes or until knife inserted near center comes out clean.

- While salmon mixture is baking, measure mayonnaise and mustard into small mixing bowl. Mix well. Set aside.

- Place the remaining egg white in small mixing bowl. Beat until stiff but not dry. Fold into mayonnaise mixture. Remove baked salmon mixture from oven. Spread mayonnaise mixture evenly over top. Return to oven and continue baking about 5 minutes longer or until topping is set. Remove from oven. Sprinkle the remaining 1 teaspoon parsley flakes over top. Cut into squares and serve immediately.

Yield:   6 servings

**VARIATIONS:**

**Tangy Topped Tuna Bake:** 2 cans (7 oz. each) solid pack white tuna, drained and flaked, may be substituted for the salmon.

**Herb-Seasoned Salmon Bake:** 2 cups Croutettes herb seasoned croutons may be substituted for the Rice Krispies cereal. Add to sour cream mixture in step 1. Let stand 10 minutes. Beat until smooth. Continue as directed on page 108.

# golden fried salmon patties

**2 eggs**

**1 cup Corn Flake Crumbs**

**1 can (15-1/2 oz.) salmon, drained, skinned, boned and flaked**

**1/2 teaspoon salt**

**1/8 teaspoon pepper**

**2 tablespoons dried parsley flakes**

**3 tablespoons finely chopped onion**

**1/4 cup milk**

**Vegetable oil or shortening (for frying)**

- In medium-size mixing bowl, beat eggs slightly. Add 1/2 cup of the Corn Flake Crumbs and remaining ingredients except oil. Mix until well combined. Shape into 12 flat patties, about 2-1/2 inches in diameter. Coat with remaining 1/2 cup Crumbs.

- Fry patties in small amount of oil in large frypan about 2 minutes on each side or until golden brown. Serve with tartar sauce or a lemon wedge, if desired.

Yield: 6 servings, 2 patties each

# corn-crisped salmon croquettes

1-1/2 cups Corn Flake Crumbs
1 can (15-1/2 oz.) salmon, drained, skinned, boned and flaked
1 cup evaporated milk
1/4 cup pickle relish
1/4 cup finely chopped celery
2 tablespoons finely chopped onion
2 tablespoons regular margarine or butter, melted

- In medium-size mixing bowl, mix together 1/2 cup of the Corn Flake Crumbs, the salmon, 1/2 cup of the milk, the relish, celery and onion. Shape mixture into 10 balls or cones.

- Dip balls in the remaining 1/2 cup milk. Coat with the remaining 1 cup Crumbs. Place in single layer in shallow baking pan. Do not crowd. Drizzle with melted margarine.

- Bake in oven at 350° F. about 35 minutes or until golden brown. Serve with a creamed vegetable sauce, if desired.

Yield:   5 servings, 2 croquettes each

# cheesy potluck casserole

2 tablespoons regular margarine or butter, melted
1/2 teaspoon paprika
2 cups Rice Krispies cereal, crushed to measure 1 cup

        *         *         *         *         *

3 tablespoons regular margarine or butter
3 tablespoons regular all-purpose flour
1-2/3 cups milk
2 cups shredded American cheese
2 cups cooked rice
1/4 cup snipped fresh parsley
1 can (7 oz.) solid pack white tuna, drained and flaked

- Combine the 2 tablespoons melted margarine with the paprika and crushed Rice Krispies cereal. Set aside for topping.

- Melt the 3 tablespoons margarine in medium-size saucepan over low heat. Stir in flour. Add milk gradually, stirring until smooth. Increase heat to medium and cook until bubbly and thickened, stirring constantly. Add cheese, stirring until melted. Remove from heat. Stir in rice, parsley and tuna. Pour into greased 2-quart casserole. Sprinkle cereal mixture evenly over top.

- Bake in oven at 350° F. about 20 minutes or until thoroughly heated and bubbly.

Yield:  6 to 8 servings

**VARIATIONS:**

1 cup cubed cooked ham, chicken or turkey may be substituted for the tuna.

# baked fish fillets

---

> **2 lbs. fish fillets, fresh or frozen**
> **3 cups Rice Krispies cereal, crushed to measure 1-1/2 cups**
> **1/2 teaspoon salt**
> **1/8 teaspoon pepper**
> **1 tablespoon dried parsley flakes**
> **1/2 cup regular margarine or butter**

- If frozen fish is used, thaw, rinse and pat dry. Set aside.

- Place crushed Rice Krispies cereal in shallow dish or pan. Stir in salt, pepper and parsley flakes. Set aside.

- Melt margarine. Pour into a second shallow dish or pan. Dip fish fillets in margarine. Coat with cereal mixture. Place in single layer in well-greased or foil-lined shallow baking pan.

- Bake in oven at 375° F. about 25 minutes or until fish flakes easily when tested with a fork. Do not cover pan or turn fish while baking.

Yield:  6 servings

# crab imperial

1 tablespoon mayonnaise or salad dressing
1/2 cup Corn Flake Crumbs

\*       \*       \*       \*       \*

1 egg
1/3 cup mayonnaise or salad dressing
1 teaspoon prepared mustard
1/2 teaspoon salt
1/8 teaspoon white pepper
3 cups cut-up, cooked crab, tendons removed
1/4 cup finely chopped green pepper
2 tablespoons chopped pimiento

- Combine the 1 tablespoon mayonnaise with the Corn Flake Crumbs. Set aside for topping.

- In medium-size mixing bowl, beat egg slightly. Stir in remaining ingredients. Portion mixture evenly into 6 greased individual shells or casseroles. Top with Crumbs mixture.

- Bake in oven at 350° F. about 20 minutes or until thoroughly heated.

Yield:  6 servings

# apple mélange salad

1/4 cup regular margarine or butter
1-1/2 cups Croutettes herb seasoned croutons
2 cans (7 oz. each) solid pack white tuna, drained and flaked
1 medium-size avocado, peeled, cut into thin strips
1 cup cubed sharp cheddar cheese
2 cups cubed apples (do not pare)
1 cup seedless green grapes
3/4 cup creamy cucumber dressing
6 lettuce cups

- Melt margarine in medium-size frypan over low heat. Add Croutettes croutons, stirring until well coated. Cook, stirring frequently, until croutons are crisped and golden. Remove from heat. Set aside.

- Place tuna, avocado, cheese, apples, grapes, dressing and 1 cup of the croutons in large mixing bowl. Toss gently to combine. Portion mixture evenly into lettuce cups. Sprinkle remaining croutons over top. Serve immediately.

Yield:  6 servings

# baked seafood salad

**2 tablespoons regular margarine or butter, melted**
**2 cups Corn Flakes cereal, crushed to measure 1 cup**

      *      *      *      *      *

**1 cup cut-up, cooked crab, tendons removed**
**1 cup cooked, deveined shrimp**
**1/2 cup finely chopped green pepper**
**1/4 cup finely chopped onion**
**1 cup thinly sliced celery**
**1 cup mayonnaise**
**1/2 teaspoon salt**
**1 teaspoon Worcestershire sauce**
**Paprika**

- Combine melted margarine with crushed Corn Flakes cereal. Set aside for topping.

- Measure remaining ingredients except paprika into medium-size mixing bowl. Stir gently until combined. Portion mixture evenly into 6 individual shells or spread in 9 x 9 x 2-inch baking pan. Top with cereal mixture. Sprinkle with paprika.

- Bake in oven at 350° F. about 30 minutes or until thoroughly heated.

Yield:  6 servings

# POULTRY

# POULTRY

Just as a Thanksgiving celebration isn't complete without the turkey, a busy Sunday is the day traditionally reserved for a fried chicken dinner. Indeed, poultry is an economical and oh-so-tasty main dish that can be prepared in countless ways.

1.  orange-stuffed roast duckling, p. 125
2.  chicken bundles, p. 120
    creamy mushroom sauce, p. 121
3.  double coated chicken, p. 119
4.  saucy chicken bake, p. 118
5.  deluxe creamed turkey, p. 127
6.  curried bran biscuits, p. 44
7.  deep-dish chicken pie, p. 122

# roast poultry

- Wash poultry, drain and dry. Turn wing tips back. Spoon prepared Croutettes stuffing (see *Stuffing Guide*) into neck and body cavities. Fasten cavities by securing skin with skewers.

- Place bird, breast side up, in roasting pan. Insert meat thermometer in inner thigh muscle. Brush skin with melted margarine or butter. Roast in oven at 325° F. until meat thermometer reaches 180° to 185°F.

- To check stuffing temperature, remove thermometer from thigh and insert in body cavity. Thermometer should register 165° F. If meat thermometer is not used, allow about 25 minutes per pound depending on size of bird. When drumstick moves up and down easily and leg joint gives readily, bird is done.

- To bake extra stuffing, spoon into buttered baking dish, cover and bake at 350° F. about 30 minutes.

# Croutettes stuffing guide

| Poultry weight | 3 to 5 lbs. | 6 to 8 lbs. | 9 to 11 lbs. | 12 to 15 lbs. | 16 to 19 lbs. | 20 lbs. and over |
|---|---|---|---|---|---|---|
| Croutettes croutons (7-oz. pkg., 7 cups) | 1/2 pkg. | 1 pkg. | 1 1/2 pkgs. | 2 pkgs. | 2 1/2 pkgs. | 3 pkgs. |
| Melted margarine or butter | 1/4 to 1/3 cup | 1/2 to 2/3 cup | 3/4 to 1 cup | 1 to 1 1/4 cups | 1 1/4 to 1 1/2 cups | 1 1/2 to 2 cups |
| Hot water or stock | 3/4 cup | 1 1/2 cups | 2 1/4 cups | 3 cups | 3 3/4 cups | 4 1/2 cups |
| **For Celery-Onion Stuffing** | | | | | | |
| Finely chopped celery | 1/4 cup | 1/2 cup | 1 cup | 1 cup | 1 1/4 cups | 1 1/2 cups |
| Chopped onions | 2 tbsps. | 1/4 cup | 1/2 cup | 1/2 cup | 2/3 cup | 3/4 cup |

For *Basic Stuffing,* pour Croutettes croutons into large mixing bowl. Add melted margarine or butter while tossing gently. Stir lightly while adding hot water or stock. (Amount of water may be varied depending on preference for a fluffy or more moist stuffing).

For *Celery-Onion Stuffing,* cook celery and onions in the melted margarine until tender before mixing with Croutettes croutons.

# baked chicken supreme

4 cups Rice Krispies cereal

1 teaspoon paprika

1 egg

3/4 cup milk

3/4 cup regular all-purpose flour

1-1/2 teaspoons salt

1/4 teaspoon pepper

1 teaspoon poultry seasoning

3 lbs. frying chicken pieces, washed and patted dry

3 tablespoons regular margarine or butter, melted

● Crush the 4 cups Rice Krispies cereal to measure 2 cups. Place in shallow dish or pan. Stir in paprika. Set aside.

● In a second shallow dish or pan, beat egg and milk slightly. Add flour, salt, pepper and poultry seasoning. Mix until smooth. Dip chicken in batter. Coat with crushed cereal. Place in single layer, skin side up, in well-greased or foil-lined shallow baking pan. Drizzle with melted margarine.

● Bake in oven at 350° F. about 1 hour or until chicken is tender. Do not cover pan or turn chicken while baking.

Yield:   6 servings

# saucy chicken bake

4 cups Croutettes herb seasoned croutons

1 can (10-3/4 oz.) condensed cream of onion soup

3/4 cup milk

2 lbs. frying chicken pieces, washed and patted dry

2 tablespoons regular margarine or butter, melted

Dried parsley flakes

- Crush the 4 cups Croutettes croutons to fine crumbs, using rolling pin or electric blender. Place in shallow dish or pan. Set aside.

- Measure 1/3 cup of the soup and 1/4 cup of the milk into a second shallow dish or pan. Stir until smooth. Dip chicken in soup mixture. Coat with crushed croutons. Place in a single layer, skin side up, in well-greased or foil-lined shallow baking pan. Drizzle with melted margarine.

- Bake in oven at 350° F. about 1 hour or until chicken is tender. Do not cover pan or turn chicken while baking.

- While chicken is baking, combine remaining soup and remaining milk in small saucepan. Cook over low heat, stirring occasionally, until mixture boils. To serve, spoon sauce over chicken. Sprinkle with parsley flakes.

Yield:  4 servings

# double coated chicken

**1-3/4 cups Corn Flake Crumbs**

**1 egg**

**1 cup milk**

**1 cup regular all-purpose flour**

**1-1/2 teaspoons salt**

**1/4 teaspoon pepper**

**3 lbs. frying chicken pieces, washed and patted dry**

**3 tablespoons regular margarine or butter, melted**

- Measure Corn Flake Crumbs into shallow dish or pan. Set aside.

- In small mixing bowl, beat egg and milk slightly. Add flour, salt and pepper. Mix until smooth. Dip chicken in batter. Coat with Crumbs. Place in single layer, skin side up, in well-greased or foil-lined shallow baking pan. Drizzle with melted margarine.

- Bake in oven at 350° F. about 1 hour or until chicken is tender. Do not cover pan or turn chicken while baking.

Yield:  6 servings

# savory chicken divan

1/3 cup regular margarine or butter
1/4 cup regular all-purpose flour
    Dash pepper
  1 can (13-3/4 oz., 1-3/4 cups) chicken broth
1/2 cup whipping cream
  3 cups Croutettes herb seasoned croutons
  1 package (10 oz.) frozen broccoli spears, cooked and drained
  8 large slices cooked chicken breasts
1/4 cup grated parmesan cheese

● Melt margarine in small saucepan over low heat. Stir in flour and pepper. Add chicken broth gradually, stirring until smooth. Increase heat to medium and cook until bubbly and thickened, stirring constantly. Remove from heat. Stir in whipping cream.

● Measure Croutettes croutons into greased 2-quart casserole. Pour half the sauce over croutons. Arrange broccoli over croutons and sauce. Top with a layer of chicken slices. Cover with remaining sauce. Sprinkle with cheese.

● Bake in oven at 350° F. about 25 minutes or until thoroughly heated.

Yield:   4 to 6 servings

# chicken bundles

  1 cup All-Bran cereal or Bran Buds cereal
1/4 cup finely chopped nuts
1/8 teaspoon pepper
1/8 teaspoon ground sage
1/8 teaspoon ground thyme
  5 tablespoons regular margarine or butter, melted
1/2 teaspoon lemon juice
  2 tablespoons finely chopped onion
  1 tablespoon chopped pimiento
  1 cup cubed cooked chicken
  1 can (8 oz.) refrigerated crescent dinner rolls

120

- In small mixing bowl, combine 1/4 cup of the All-Bran cereal, 2 table-spoons of the nuts, the pepper, sage, thyme, 3 tablespoons of the melted margarine, the lemon juice, onion, pimiento and chicken. Mix well. Set aside for filling.

- Crush the remaining 3/4 cup cereal to coarse crumbs and mix with the re-maining 2 tablespoons nuts. Set aside for coating.

- Separate dinner rolls dough into 4 squares (2 triangles each). Firmly press perforations to seal. Place about 1/3 cup filling in center of each square. Gather corners together, pinching to seal. Brush bundles with the remaining 2 tablespoons melted margarine. Roll in the coating mixture, adding additional cereal if needed. Place on ungreased baking sheet.

- Bake in oven at 350° F. about 25 minutes or until lightly browned and pastry is done. Serve with *Creamy Mushroom Sauce.*

Yield:   4 servings

# creamy mushroom sauce

**2 tablespoons regular margarine or butter**
**1 tablespoon regular all-purpose flour**
**1/4 teaspoon salt**
**1/4 teaspoon pepper**
**1/2 teaspoon dried parsley flakes**
**2/3 cup milk**
**1 jar (2-1/2 oz.) sliced mushrooms, drained**
**1/2 cup dairy sour cream**

- Melt margarine in small saucepan over low heat. Stir in flour, salt, pepper and parsley flakes. Add milk gradually, stirring until smooth. Stir in mushrooms.

- Increase heat to medium and cook until bubbly and thickened, stirring constantly. Stir in sour cream. Cook until heated through. Do not boil.

Yield:   1-1/2 cups

# deep-dish chicken pie

  2 cups cubed cooked chicken
  1 cup thinly sliced carrots
  1 cup thinly sliced potato (1 medium-size)
  1 cup boiled whole onions, drained
1/2 cup peas
  1 can (10-3/4 oz.) condensed cream of mushroom soup
1/2 cup milk
1/2 teaspoon salt
1/8 teaspoon pepper
1/4 teaspoon poultry seasoning

          *          *          *          *          *

  1 package (11 oz.) pie crust mix
1/2 cup Corn Flake Crumbs
  7 tablespoons cold water

- In greased 12 x 7-1/2 x 2-inch (2-quart) glass baking dish, stir together chicken, carrots, potato, onions and peas. In small mixing bowl, stir together soup, milk, salt, pepper and poultry seasoning. Pour evenly over chicken mixture. Set aside.

- In medium-size mixing bowl, stir together pie crust mix and Corn Flake Crumbs. Add water, stirring with fork, until dough holds together. Add 1 to 2 teaspoons additional water if needed. On floured surface, roll out crust to fit baking dish, 1/8 inch thick. Cut steam slits in crust. Place over chicken mixture.

- Bake in oven at 375° F. about 1 hour or until crust is lightly browned and vegetables are tender. Test doneness by inserting tip of knife into one of the steam slits.

Yield:   8 servings

NOTE:   If desired, roll out extra dough to make small pastry cutouts to decorate pie. Arrange on chicken pie crust before baking.

# stuffing amandine

**2 eggs**
**1 can (13-3/4 oz., 1-3/4 cups) chicken broth**
**1/2 package (3-1/2 cups) Croutettes herb seasoned croutons**
**1/4 cup finely chopped almonds**

- In large mixing bowl, beat eggs slightly. Stir in chicken broth. Add Croutettes croutons and almonds, tossing lightly until croutons are evenly and thoroughly moistened. Spoon into well-greased 8 x 8 x 2-inch baking pan, pressing lightly.
- Bake in oven at 350° F. about 30 minutes or until set. Cut into squares and serve with *Chicken and Mushroom Sauce.*

Yield:   6 servings

# chicken and mushroom sauce

**1/3 cup regular margarine or butter**
**1/3 cup regular all-purpose flour**
**1 teaspoon salt**
**3 cups milk**
**2 cups cubed cooked chicken**
**1 can (4 oz.) mushroom stems and pieces, drained**
**2 tablespoons chopped pimiento**
**2 tablespoons snipped fresh parsley**

- Melt margarine in medium-size saucepan over low heat. Stir in flour and salt. Add milk gradually, stirring until smooth. Stir in remaining ingredients.
- Increase heat to medium and cook until bubbly and thickened, stirring constantly.

Yield:   5 cups

# crunchy baked chicken variations

Wash 3 lbs. frying chicken pieces. Pat dry. For any of the following varia-tions, **Dip** chicken in liquid mixture. **Coat** evenly with Crumbs mixture. Place in single layer, skin side up, in well-greased or foil-lined shallow baking pan. Drizzle with 3 tablespoons melted margarine or butter, if desired. **Bake** in oven at 350° F. about 1 hour or until chicken is tender. Do not cover pan or turn chicken while baking.
Yield:   6 servings

### Corn–Crisped Chicken*

**Dip** in 1/2 cup evaporated milk. **Coat** with mixture of 1 cup Corn Flake Crumbs, 1 teaspoon salt and 1/8 teaspoon pepper.

### California Crusty Chicken

**Dip** in mixture of 1/4 cup melted margarine or butter, 3 tablespoons lemon juice and 1 teaspoon grated lemon peel. **Coat** with mixture of 1-1/4 cups Corn Flake Crumbs, 1-1/2 teaspoons salt and 1/4 teaspoon pepper.

### Baked Chicken Italiano

**Dip** in 1/2 cup Italian-style salad dressing. **Coat** with 1-1/4 cups Corn Flake Crumbs. If desired, marinate chicken in dressing for at least 1 hour.

### Oven–Fried Chicken

**Dip** in mixture of 1 slightly beaten egg and 2 tablespoons milk. **Coat** with mixture of 1-1/4 cups Corn Flake Crumbs, 1-1/2 teaspoons salt and 1/4 teaspoon pepper.

### Parmesan Crisped Chicken

**Dip** in mixture of 1 slightly beaten egg and 2 tablespoons milk. **Coat** with mixture of 3/4 cup Corn Flake Crumbs, 1-1/2 teaspoons salt, 1/4 teaspoon pepper and 1/2 cup grated parmesan cheese.

### Zesty Crisped Chicken

**Dip** in mixture of 1 slightly beaten egg and 1/4 cup soy sauce. **Coat** with 1-1/4 cups Corn Flake Crumbs.

*See page 185 for microwave directions.

# orange-stuffed roast duckling

**1 duckling (4 to 5 lbs.), washed and patted dry**
  **Salt**
**1/4 cup regular margarine or butter**
**3/4 cup finely chopped celery**
  **1 can (11 oz.) mandarin orange segments, drained,**
  **reserving syrup**
**1/2 package (3-1/2 cups) Croutettes herb seasoned croutons**
  **Orange flavored liqueur**
  **2 teaspoons cornstarch**
  **2 teaspoons grated lemon peel**
  **1 tablespoon lemon juice**

● Remove wing tips from duckling up to first joint. Sprinkle inside cavity with salt. Set aside.

● Melt margarine in small frypan. Add celery and cook over low heat until tender. Remove from heat. Stir in 1/4 cup of the reserved orange syrup. (Save remaining syrup.) Set aside.

● Measure Croutettes croutons into large mixing bowl. Add drained orange segments, mixing lightly. While tossing gently, add celery mixture. Lightly stuff duckling. Close opening with skewers and tie legs together with string. Prick skin several times with a fork to allow fat to drain slowly, self-basting the duckling. Place on rack, breast side up, in roasting pan.

● Roast duckling in oven at 325° F. for 2 to 2-1/2 hours or until tender (about 30 minutes per pound). If necessary, cover duckling lightly with foil during last hour to prevent over-browning.

● For glaze, add orange flavored liqueur to remaining syrup to measure 2/3 cup. In small saucepan, stir together syrup mixture, cornstarch, lemon peel and lemon juice. Cook over medium heat until thickened and clear, stirring frequently. Remove from heat. Brush over duckling several times during roasting.

Yield:   4 servings

# chicken Hawaiian

    3 lbs. frying chicken pieces, washed and patted dry
    1 teaspoon salt
    1 egg, slightly beaten
    1/3 cup frozen pineapple-orange juice concentrate, thawed
    1 cup Corn Flake Crumbs
    1/2 cup shredded coconut
    1/2 teaspoon curry powder
    3 tablespoons regular margarine or butter, melted

● Place chicken in single layer in shallow pan. Sprinkle with salt. Stir together egg and juice concentrate. Pour over chicken. Cover and chill at least 1 hour, turning pieces several times.

● Measure Corn Flake Crumbs into shallow dish or pan. Stir in coconut and curry powder. Drain chicken pieces slightly. Coat with Crumbs mixture. Place in single layer, skin side up, in well-greased or foil-lined shallow baking pan. Drizzle with melted margarine.

● Bake in oven at 350° F. about 1 hour or until chicken is tender. Do not cover pan or turn chicken while baking. Garnish with pineapple rings dipped in coconut, if desired.

Yield:   6 servings

# chicken elegante

    3 lbs. frying chicken pieces, washed and patted dry
  2/3 cup water
    2 tablespoons vegetable oil
    2 tablespoons bourbon whiskey
    2 tablespoons aromatic bitters
    2 tablespoons lemon juice
1-1/2 cups Corn Flake Crumbs
    1 teaspoon salt
    1 teaspoon garlic salt
    1 egg
  3/4 cup regular all-purpose flour
    3 tablespoons regular margarine or butter, melted

- Place chicken in single layer in shallow pan. In small mixing bowl, stir together water, oil, whiskey, bitters and lemon juice. Pour over chicken. Cover and chill at least 2 hours, turning pieces several times. Drain chicken, reserving marinade.

- Measure Corn Flake Crumbs into shallow dish or pan. Stir in salt and garlic salt. Set aside.

- In small mixing bowl, beat egg slightly. Stir in reserved marinade. Add flour, mixing until smooth. Dip chicken in batter. Coat with Crumbs mixture. Place in single layer, skin side up, in well-greased or foil-lined shallow baking pan. Drizzle with melted margarine.

- Bake in oven at 350° F. about 1 hour or until chicken is tender. Do not cover pan or turn chicken while baking.

Yield: 6 servings

# deluxe creamed turkey

3 tablespoons regular margarine or butter
1/4 cup finely chopped green pepper
1/4 cup finely chopped onion
1 can (10-3/4 oz.) condensed cream of mushroom soup
1 carton (8 oz., 1 cup) dairy sour cream
1/8 teaspoon pepper
2 cups cubed cooked turkey
1 package (10 oz.) frozen peas, cooked and drained

- Melt margarine in large saucepan. Add green pepper and onion. Cook over low heat until tender.

- Add soup, sour cream and pepper, stirring until smooth. Gently stir in turkey and peas. Cook until thoroughly heated. Serve over *Curried Bran Biscuits* (see page 44).

Yield: 6 servings

# turkey jubilee

      1 cup Corn Flakes cereal

      4 tablespoons regular margarine or butter

  1/4 cup regular all-purpose flour

  1/4 teaspoon salt

      Dash pepper

  3/4 cup chicken or turkey broth or stock

      1 cup evaporated milk

1-1/2 cups cubed cooked turkey

      1 jar (2-1/2 oz.) sliced mushrooms, undrained

\*      \*      \*      \*      \*

      1 cup Corn Flakes cereal

      1 cup regular all-purpose flour

      2 teaspoons baking powder

  1/2 teaspoon salt

      1 egg

  2/3 cup evaporated milk

  1/2 cup shredded sharp cheddar cheese

- Crush the 1 cup Corn Flakes cereal to measure 1/2 cup. Melt 1 tablespoon of the margarine in small saucepan. Remove from heat. Add crushed cereal, stirring until well coated. Set aside.

- Melt the remaining 3 tablespoons margarine in medium-size saucepan over low heat. Stir in the 1/4 cup flour, the 1/4 teaspoon salt and the pepper. Add chicken or turkey broth and the 1 cup evaporated milk gradually, stirring until smooth. Increase heat to medium and cook until bubbly and thickened, stirring constantly. Remove from heat. Stir in turkey and mushrooms. Set aside.

- Crush the remaining 1 cup cereal to measure 1/2 cup. Stir together crushed cereal, the 1 cup flour, the baking powder and the 1/2 teaspoon salt. Set aside.

- In medium-size mixing bowl, beat egg slightly. Stir in the 2/3 cup evaporated milk and the cheese. Add flour mixture, stirring only until combined. Spread evenly in well-greased 8 x 8 x 2-inch (1-1/2-quart) glass baking dish. Spoon turkey mixture over batter. Sprinkle reserved cereal evenly over top.

● Bake in oven at 350° F. about 30 minutes or until bubbly around edges.

Yield:   6 servings

NOTE:   The total amount of evaporated milk used in this recipe is contained in one 13-oz. can.

# cheesy potluck casserole

Use 1 cup cubed cooked chicken or turkey in place of tuna in the recipe for *Cheesy Potluck Casserole* that appears on page 110.

# DESSERTS

# DESSERTS

Dessert can be the fitting conclusion to a nourishing meal or the pièce de résistance for a special get-together. From a simple pudding or fruit crumble to a multi-layered cake, attractively-served and carefully-prepared desserts can glamorize and complement even the simplest occasion.

| | | | |
|---|---|---|---|
| 1. | sweet chocolate cake, p. 148 | 5. | key lime pie, p. 153 |
| 2. | strawberry Danish tarts, p. 136 | 6. | fruit empanadas, p. 145 |
| 3. | apricot fluff pie, p. 142 | 7. | almond crunch pudding, p. 134 |
| 4. | crunchy ice cream sandwiches, p. 140 | 8. | Danish dessert cake, p. 154 |

# French cherry dessert

1/2 cup regular margarine or butter, softened

   3 tablespoons sifted confectioners' sugar

1/2 cup regular all-purpose flour

1/2 cup Corn Flake Crumbs

      *        *        *        *        *

1/4 cup regular all-purpose flour

1/2 teaspoon baking powder

1/4 teaspoon salt

   2 eggs

   1 cup granulated sugar

   1 teaspoon vanilla flavoring

1/2 cup coarsely chopped nuts

1/2 cup flaked coconut

1/2 cup finely chopped maraschino cherries

   Whipped topping or vanilla ice cream

- In small mixing bowl, beat margarine and confectioners' sugar until smooth and creamy. Stir in the 1/2 cup flour and the Corn Flake Crumbs. Spread mixture evenly in bottom of 8 x 8 x 2-inch baking pan.

- Bake in oven at 325° F. about 20 minutes or until crust springs back when lightly touched. Remove from oven.

- Stir together the 1/4 cup flour, the baking powder and salt. Set aside.

- In medium-size mixing bowl, beat eggs slightly. Stir in granulated sugar and vanilla. Add flour mixture, mixing until well combined. Stir in nuts, coconut and cherries. Spread mixture over crust.

- Bake in oven at 325° F. about 30 minutes or until lightly browned. Cool. Cut into squares and serve with whipped topping or a small scoop of vanilla ice cream.

Yield:  9 servings

See page 199 for microwave directions.

133

# apple crisp

    1 cup Cracklin' Bran cereal
1/2 cup regular all-purpose flour
3/4 teaspoon ground cinnamon
3/4 teaspoon ground nutmeg
2/3 cup firmly packed brown sugar
1/3 cup regular margarine or butter, softened
    4 cups sliced, pared tart apples

- Using rolling pin, crush the 1 cup Cracklin' Bran cereal to measure 1/2 cup. Place in medium-size mixing bowl. Add flour, cinnamon, nutmeg and sugar, mixing until well combined. Add margarine, mixing until crumbly.

- Place apples in greased 8 x 8 x 2-inch baking pan. Sprinkle cereal mixture evenly over top.

- Bake in oven at 375° F. about 30 minutes or until apples are tender and topping is golden brown. Serve warm with half-and-half or ice cream, if desired.

Yield:   6 servings

# almond crunch pudding

    1 tablespoon regular margarine or butter
3/4 cup coarsely chopped almonds
1/4 cup honey
    1 tablespoon grated orange peel
    Dash salt
1-1/2 cups Corn Flakes cereal

        *           *           *           *           *

    1 cup cold milk
    1 package (3-5/8 oz.) vanilla instant pudding mix
1/2 pint (1 cup) whipping cream, whipped

134

- Melt margarine in medium-size frypan. Add almonds. Cook over medium heat, stirring frequently, until almonds are lightly browned. Reduce heat to low. Add honey, orange peel and salt. Cook 2 minutes longer, stirring constantly. Remove from heat. Add Corn Flakes cereal, stirring until well coated. Spread on waxed paper or buttered baking sheet. Cool completely. Break into small pieces. Set aside.

- Pour milk into small mixing bowl. Add pudding mix. Beat slowly with rotary beater or at lowest speed of electric mixer for 2 minutes. Fold in whipped cream.

- For each serving, place a spoonful of cereal mixture in dessert dish. Top with pudding mixture. Sprinkle with additional cereal mixture.

Yield:   6 servings

NOTE:   Extra cereal mixture may be stored in tightly covered container.

# all-American party pudding

**1/3 cup seedless raisins**

  **20 Frosted Mini-Wheats biscuits or Toasted Mini-Wheats biscuits**

    **3 eggs**

**1/2 cup granulated sugar or firmly packed brown sugar**

**1/2 teaspoon salt**

    **1 teaspoon vanilla flavoring**

    **2 tablespoons regular margarine or butter**

    **2 cups milk**

- Sprinkle raisins evenly in ungreased 10 x 6 x 2-inch (1-1/2-quart) glass baking dish. Place Frosted Mini-Wheats biscuits, frosted side up, in single layer over raisins. Set aside.

- In medium-size mixing bowl, beat eggs until foamy. Add sugar, salt, vanilla and margarine, mixing only until combined. Scald milk. Gradually add hot milk to egg mixture, stirring constantly until margarine is melted. Pour milk mixture evenly over biscuits.

- Bake in oven at 300° F. about 1 hour or until knife inserted near center comes out clean. Cut into squares. Serve warm with half-and-half or ice cream.

Yield:   6 servings

See page 194 for microwave directions.

# strawberry Danish tarts

2 cups regular all-purpose flour

1 teaspoon salt

3/4 cup shortening

1/4 cup boiling water

1 tablespoon milk

\*         \*         \*         \*         \*

2 cups cold water

1 package (4-3/4 oz.) strawberry flavor Junket Danish Dessert

1-1/2 cups sliced strawberries

1 package (8 oz.) cream cheese, softened

3 tablespoons sugar

1/8 teaspoon vanilla flavoring

- For tart shells, stir together flour and salt. Set aside.

- Measure shortening, boiling water and milk into small bowl of electric mixer. Beat at medium speed until smooth and thick and mixture holds soft peaks.

- Add flour mixture, stirring quickly with fork until dough clings together. Work dough into a smooth ball. Divide ball into 4 parts. Roll each to 1/8-inch thickness on lightly floured surface. Cut out 4 to 5 circles, 4 inches in diameter, from each. Fit over backs of 2-1/2-inch muffin-pan cups, pinching into about 6 pleats. Prick each tart several times with fork.

- Bake in oven at 450° F. about 7 minutes or until pastry is lightly browned. Cool slightly. Carefully remove from muffin-pan cups.

- For fruit filling, measure cold water into medium-size saucepan. Stir in Danish Dessert. Bring to full boil over medium heat. Boil 1 minute, stirring constantly. Remove from heat. Cool completely. Fold in strawberries. Set aside.

- In small mixing bowl, beat cream cheese, sugar and vanilla until light and fluffy. Gently spread on bottom and sides of cooled tart shells. Fill tarts with strawberry mixture. Chill 3 to 4 hours.

Yield:  about 1-1/2 dozen

# fresh apple cake

**1-1/2 cups regular all-purpose flour**

    **2 teaspoons baking soda**

  **1/2 teaspoon salt**

    **1 teaspoon ground cinnamon**

    **1 teaspoon ground nutmeg**

  **1/2 cup regular margarine or butter, softened**

    **1 cup sugar**

    **2 eggs**

    **4 cups finely chopped, pared apples**

    **1 cup All-Bran cereal or Bran Buds cereal**

- Stir together flour, soda, salt, cinnamon and nutmeg. Set aside.

- Beat margarine and sugar until light and fluffy. Add eggs. Beat well. Stir in apples, All-Bran cereal and flour mixture. Spread in well-greased 9 x 9 x 2-inch baking pan.

- Bake in oven at 350° F. about 1 hour or until cake begins to pull away from sides of pan. Cool completely. Spread with *Fluffy Frosting.* Cut into squares to serve.

Yield:   12 servings

# fluffy frosting

    **1 tablespoon regular all-purpose flour**

  **1/4 cup milk**

  **1/4 cup regular margarine or butter, softened**

  **1/4 cup sugar**

- Measure flour into small saucepan. Add milk gradually, stirring until smooth. Cook over low heat until bubbly and thickened, stirring constantly. Remove from heat. Cool completely.

- In small mixing bowl, beat margarine and sugar until light and fluffy. Add cooled flour mixture and beat until light and of spreading consistency.

NOTE:   If mixture appears curdled, continue beating until smooth.

# frosty holiday pie

1/4 cup regular margarine or butter

1/4 cup corn syrup

1/2 cup semi-sweet chocolate morsels

2 cups Rice Krispies cereal

4 packages (3 oz. each) cream cheese, softened

3/4 cup sugar

2 tablespoons brandy

1/2 cup quartered maraschino cherries

1/2 cup chopped almonds

2-1/4 cups whipped topping

- Melt margarine, corn syrup and chocolate morsels together in medium-size saucepan over low heat, stirring constantly until smooth. Remove from heat. Add Rice Krispies cereal, stirring until well coated. With back of spoon, gently press mixture evenly around sides and in bottom of buttered 9-inch pie pan to form crust. Chill.

- In large mixing bowl, beat cream cheese until smooth. Gradually beat in sugar. Stir in brandy. Fold in cherries, almonds and whipped topping. Spoon filling into chilled crust. Garnish with additional maraschino cherries, halved, and toasted slivered almonds, if desired. Freeze at least 4 hours.

Yield:  one 9-inch pie

NOTE:  For easier cutting, let stand at room temperature about 15 minutes before serving.

# no-roll pie crust

1-1/4 cups regular all-purpose flour

1/2 teaspoon salt

1 tablespoon sugar

1/2 cup Corn Flake Crumbs

1/3 cup vegetable oil

2 tablespoons cold water

- Measure flour, salt, sugar and Corn Flake Crumbs into medium-size mixing bowl. Add oil and water, stirring with fork until well mixed.

- With back of spoon, press mixture evenly and firmly around sides and in bottom of 9-inch pie pan to form crust.

- Fill and bake pie as directed in individual recipe. Or for baked crust, prick bottom and sides with a fork. Bake in oven at 450° F. about 10 minutes or until lightly browned. Cool completely. Use for any refrigerated or frozen filling.

Yield: one 9-inch pie crust

# easy bran pie crust

**3/4 cup All-Bran cereal or Bran Buds cereal**
**1 cup regular all-purpose flour**
**1/2 cup regular margarine or butter**
**2 tablespoons milk**

- Stir All-Bran cereal and flour together in medium-size mixing bowl. Cut in margarine until mixture resembles coarse meal.

- Add milk, stirring until entire mixture is moistened. Dough will seem slightly crumbly. With back of spoon, press mixture evenly and firmly around sides and in bottom of 9-inch pie pan to form crust.

- Fill and bake pie as directed in individual recipe. Or for baked crust, prick bottom and sides with a fork. Bake in oven at 400° F. about 12 minutes or until lightly browned. Cool completely. Use for any refrigerated or frozen filling.

Yield: one 9-inch pie crust

# crunchy ice cream sandwiches

        1/2 cup light corn syrup
        1/2 cup peanut butter
          4 cups Rice Krispies cereal
          1 pint ice cream, cut into 6 slices

- In medium-size mixing bowl, stir together corn syrup and peanut butter. Add Rice Krispies cereal. Stir until well coated.

- Press mixture evenly in buttered 13 x 9 x 2-inch pan. Place in freezer or coldest part of refrigerator until firm.

- Cut cereal mixture into twelve 3-inch squares. Sandwich a slice of ice cream between 2 squares, making 6 sandwiches. Wrap individually in foil. Store in freezer until needed.

Yield:   6 servings

# coco-peanut ice cream sundaes

          3 tablespoons regular margarine or butter
        1/4 cup firmly packed brown sugar
        1/2 cup flaked coconut
        1/2 cup salted cocktail peanuts
          2 cups Product 19 multivitamin and iron supplement cereal
            Vanilla ice cream
            Butterscotch ice cream topping

- Melt margarine in medium-size saucepan. Stir in sugar. Cook over medium heat, stirring constantly, until mixture comes to a full boil. Remove from heat. Add coconut, peanuts and Product 19 supplement cereal. Stir until well coated.

- Spread on waxed paper or buttered baking sheet. Cool completely. Top individual sevings of ice cream with Butterscotch ice cream topping. Sprinkle with *Coco-Peanut* mixture.

Yield:   3 cups topping

NOTE:   Extra topping may be stored in refrigerator in tightly covered container.

*Coco-Peanut Ice Cream Crepes:* Prepare dessert crepes according to directions for use of individual crepe pan. For each serving, top crepe with a small scoop of vanilla ice cream. Sprinkle with *Coco-Peanut* mixture. Fold sides of crepe over ice cream. Sprinkle with additional *Coco-Peanut* mixture. Top with Butterscotch ice cream topping.

# easy Pop-Tarts crumble

**4 brown sugar-cinnamon Frosted Pop-Tarts pastries**
**3 tablespoons regular margarine or butter, melted**
**1 can (1 lb. 5 oz.) apple or blueberry pie filling**
**1 tablespoon lemon juice**
**1/2 teaspoon ground cinnamon**

● Crumble Pop-Tarts pastries into small pieces. Place in medium-size mixing bowl. Toss with melted margarine. Set aside.

● In 8 x 8 x 2-inch (1-1/2-quart) glass baking dish, stir together pie filling, lemon juice and cinnamon. Sprinkle crumbled pastries mixture evenly over top.

● Bake in oven at 350° F. about 25 minutes or until bubbly. Serve warm with whipped topping or ice cream, if desired.

Yield:   6 servings

VARIATIONS:

Cherry or peach pie filling may be substituted for the apple or blueberry pie filling. The following flavors of Frosted Pop-Tarts pastries may be used in place of the brown sugar-cinnamon pastries:

|  |  |
|---|---|
| blueberry | Dutch apple |
| cherry | raspberry |
| Concord grape | strawberry |

See page 195 for microwave directions.

# apricot fluff pie

**2 tablespoons regular margarine or butter**
**1/4 cup corn syrup**
**1 package (6 oz., 1 cup) semi-sweet chocolate morsels**
**2 cups Special K cereal**

\*    \*    \*    \*    \*

**1 can (17 oz.) apricot halves, well drained, reserving syrup**
**1 package (3 oz.) orange flavor gelatin**
**1 pint (2 cups) whipping cream**

● Melt margarine, corn syrup and chocolate morsels together in medium-size saucepan over low heat, stirring constantly until smooth. Remove from heat. Add Special K cereal, stirring until well coated. With back of spoon, press mixture evenly around sides and in bottom of buttered 8 or 9-inch pie pan to form crust. Chill.

● Reserve 8 apricot halves for top of pie. Cut remaining halves into small pieces for filling. Set aside.

● Measure 1 cup of the reserved apricot syrup into small saucepan. Bring to boil. Combine hot syrup with gelatin in small mixing bowl, stirring until dissolved. Chill until gelatin is consistency of unbeaten egg whites. Meanwhile, place whipping cream in large mixing bowl. Beat until stiff peaks form. Set aside.

● Whip chilled gelatin until thick and foamy and double in volume. Gently fold whipped gelatin and apricot pieces into whipped cream. Spoon filling into pie crust. Chill 1 hour or until set. Arrange reserved apricots, whole or cut in half, on pie just before serving. Garnish with additional whipped cream, if desired.

Yield:   one 8 or 9-inch pie

NOTE:   To cut pie easily, place hot wet towel under bottom and around sides of pan. Allow to stand a few minutes.

# carrot cake

                1 cup regular all-purpose flour
        1-1/2 teaspoons baking powder
            1/2 teaspoon salt
                1 teaspoon ground cinnamon
        1/8 teaspoon ground ginger
                2 eggs
                1 cup firmly packed brown sugar
        1/2 cup vegetable oil
        1-1/2 cups grated raw carrots
                2 cups Raisin Bran cereal
        1/2 cup chopped walnuts

- Stir together flour, baking powder, salt, cinnamon and ginger. Set aside.

- In large mixing bowl, beat eggs slightly. Stir in sugar and oil. Add carrots and Raisin Bran cereal. Mix well. Let stand 10 minutes.

- Add flour mixture and walnuts. Mix until well combined. Pour into greased 8 x 8 x 2-inch baking pan.

- Bake in oven at 350° F. about 45 minutes or until wooden pick inserted near center comes out clean. Cool completely. Spread with *Cream Cheese Frosting.*

Yield:  9 servings

# cream cheese frosting

                1 package (3 oz.) cream cheese, softened
                1 tablespoon regular margarine or butter, softened
                1 teaspoon vanilla flavoring
        1-1/2 cups sifted confectioners' sugar
            Milk, if needed

- In small mixing bowl, beat cream cheese, margarine and vanilla until light and fluffy. Gradually add sugar, beating until fluffy and of spreading consistency. If mixture is too thick, add 1 to 2 teaspoons milk.

1/2 cup regular margarine or butter

   3 cups Rice Krispies cereal, crushed to measure 1-1/2 cups

1/4 cup sugar

1/2 teaspoon ground cinnamon

   \*          \*          \*          \*          \*

   4 packages (3 oz. each) cream cheese, softened

   2 eggs

   1 teaspoon vanilla flavoring

1/3 cup sugar

   1 teaspoon lemon juice

   \*          \*          \*          \*          \*

   1 carton (8 oz., 1 cup) dairy sour cream

   2 tablespoons sugar

   \*          \*          \*          \*          \*

   1 can (1 lb. 5 oz.) cherry pie filling

   1 teaspoon lemon juice

● Melt margarine in small saucepan. Remove from heat. Stir in crushed Rice Krispies cereal, the 1/4 cup sugar and the cinnamon. With back of spoon, press mixture evenly and firmly around sides and in bottom of 9-inch pie pan to form crust. Set aside.

● In large mixing bowl, beat cream cheese until smooth. Add eggs, vanilla, the 1/3 cup sugar and the 1 teaspoon lemon juice, mixing until well combined. Pour mixure into crust. Bake in oven at 375° F. about 20 minutes or until set.

● While pie is baking, stir together sour cream and the 2 tablespoons sugar. Remove pie from oven. Spread sour cream mixture over top. Return to oven. Bake 5 minutes longer. Remove from oven. Cool.

● Stir together pie filling and the remaining 1 teaspoon lemon juice. Spread over top of cooled pie. Chill thoroughly.

Yield:   one 9-inch pie

# fruit empanadas

1/2 cup seedless raisins

1/2 cup finely cut, pitted dates

1/2 cup chopped nuts

   2 tablespoons orange marmalade

1/2 cup Corn Flake Crumbs

1-1/2 cups regular all-purpose flour

   1 teaspoon baking powder

1/2 teaspoon salt

1/3 cup shortening

1/2 cup milk

   Vegetable oil or shortening (for frying)

- For filling, mix together raisins, dates, nuts and marmalade in small mixing bowl. Set aside.

- Stir together Corn Flake Crumbs, flour, baking powder and salt in medium-size mixing bowl. Cut in shortening until mixture resembles coarse meal. Add milk. Mix with fork until dough holds together. Add 1 to 2 teaspoons additional milk, if needed.

- Gather dough into ball and knead gently a few times. On lightly floured surface, roll dough to 1/8-inch thickness. Cut into 4-inch circles with floured cookie cutter. Top each with 1 tablespoon filling. Moisten edge with water. Fold in half and press edges to seal, using the tines of a fork. Reroll trimmings, cut and fill.

- Heat 1/2 to 1 inch of oil in large frypan to 370° F. Lower 4 to 5 empanadas into hot oil. Fry 1 minute on each side or until golden brown. Drain on absorbent paper. Serve warm or cooled. Dust with confectioners' sugar, if desired.

Yield:  16 pastries

# shoofly pie

3/4 cup Corn Flake Crumbs
3/4 cup regular all-purpose flour
1 teaspoon baking powder
1/2 teaspoon ground cinnamon
1/8 teaspoon ground nutmeg
1/8 teaspoon ground ginger
1/8 teaspoon ground cloves
1/2 cup firmly packed brown sugar
2 tablespoons shortening
1/2 cup light molasses
3/4 cup water
3/4 teaspoon baking soda
1 unbaked 9-inch pie crust (see pages 138 and 139)

● Measure Corn Flake Crumbs, flour, baking powder, cinnamon, nutmeg, ginger, cloves and sugar into medium-size mixing bowl. Cut in shortening until mixture resembles coarse meal.

● In small mixing bowl, combine molasses, water and soda. Pour one-third of the molasses mixture into unbaked pie crust. Top with one-third of the Crumbs mixture. Repeat twice, ending with Crumbs.

● Bake in oven at 350° F. about 30 minutes or until filling is set. Cool completely before serving.

Yield: one 9-inch pie

# date 'n honey pie

1/4 cup regular margarine or butter, softened
1/3 cup honey
2/3 cup corn syrup
3 eggs
1 teaspoon vanilla flavoring
3/4 cup All-Bran or Bran Buds cereal
3/4 cup cut, pitted dates
1 unbaked 9-inch pie crust (see pages 138 and 139)

- In large mixing bowl, beat margarine, honey and corn syrup until well blended. Add eggs. Beat until smooth. Stir in vanilla, All-Bran cereal and dates. Pour into unbaked pie crust.

- Bake in oven at 350° F. about 55 minutes or until center is set. Cool completely before cutting. Top each serving with ice cream or whipped topping, if desired.

Yield:   one 9-inch pie

See page 193 for microwave directions.

# strawberry pie

**1-3/4 cups cold water**
 **1 package (4-3/4 oz.) strawberry flavor Junket Danish Dessert**
 **4 cups sliced fresh strawberries**
 **1 baked 9-inch pie crust (see pages 138, 139 and 197)**
 **2 packages (3 oz. each) cream cheese, softened**
 **2 tablespoons honey**
 **1 tablespoon toasted slivered almonds**

- Measure cold water into medium-size saucepan. Stir in Danish Dessert. Bring to full boil over medium heat. Boil 1 minute, stirring constantly. Remove from heat. Cool completely.

- Fold strawberries into cooled Danish Dessert. Spoon into baked pie crust. Chill 3 to 4 hours or until firm.

- In small mixing bowl, beat cream cheese and honey until smooth and fluffy. At serving time, garnish pie with spoonfuls of cream cheese mixture. Sprinkle with almonds.

Yield:   one 9-inch pie

# sweet chocolate cake

**1/2 cup water**
   **1 bar (4 oz.) sweet cooking chocolate**
   **2 cups regular all-purpose flour**
   **1 teaspoon baking soda**
**1/2 teaspoon salt**
   **1 cup All-Bran cereal or Bran Buds cereal**
   **1 cup regular margarine or butter, softened**
   **2 cups sugar**
   **4 eggs, separated**
   **1 teaspoon vanilla flavoring**
   **1 cup buttermilk**

- Combine water and chocolate in small saucepan. Cook over low heat, stirring constantly, until chocolate melts. Set aside to cool.

- Stir together flour, soda, salt and All-Bran cereal. Set aside.

- In large mixing bowl, beat margarine and sugar until light and fluffy. Add egg yolks, 1 at a time, beating well after each addition. Add chocolate mixture and vanilla. Mix well. Add flour mixture alternately with buttermilk, mixing until combined after each addition.

- In small mixing bowl, beat egg whites until soft peaks form. Fold into batter. Pour into 3 greased and floured 8-inch round cake pans.

- Bake in oven at 350° F. about 35 minutes or until wooden pick inserted near center comes out clean. Cool completely. Remove from pans. Spread *Coconut Pecan Frosting* between layers and on top and sides of cake.

Yield:   8 to 10 servings

# coconut pecan frosting

1 cup evaporated milk
1 cup sugar
3 egg yolks
1/2 cup regular margarine or butter
1 teaspoon vanilla flavoring
1 can (3-1/2 oz., 1-1/3 cups) flaked coconut
1 cup chopped pecans

- Combine evaporated milk, sugar, egg yolks, margarine and vanilla in small saucepan. Cook over medium heat, stirring constantly, until mixture thickens. Remove from heat. Stir in coconut and pecans. Cool, stirring occasionally, until thick enough to spread.

# bran custard surprise

3 eggs
2 cups milk
1/8 teaspoon salt
1/8 teaspoon ground nutmeg
1/2 cup sugar
1 teaspoon vanilla flavoring
1 cup Cracklin' Bran cereal
1/3 cup seedless raisins

- In medium-size mixing bowl, beat eggs until foamy. Stir in remaining ingredients. Portion evenly into 6 buttered 6-ounce custard cups or pour into buttered 10 x 6 x 2-inch (1-1/2-quart) glass baking dish.
- Place in large baking pan and fill with about 1 inch of hot water. Bake in oven at 375° F. about 45 minutes or until knife inserted near center comes out clean. Serve warm with ice cream or whipped topping, if desired.

Yield: 6 servings

See page 196 for microwave directions.

# buttery apple squares

2 cups Rice Krispies cereal

1-1/3 cups regular all-purpose flour

1/2 teaspoon salt

2/3 cup regular margarine or butter

1/4 cup milk

    \*      \*      \*      \*      \*

2 tablespoons regular all-purpose flour

1/4 teaspoon ground cinnamon

1/8 teaspoon ground nutmeg

3/4 cup sugar

5 cups sliced, pared tart apples (about 1-1/2 lbs.)

1 tablespoon lemon juice

Confectioners' Sugar Glaze (see page 151)

- Crush Rice Krispies cereal to fine crumbs. In medium-size mixing bowl, stir together crushed cereal, the 1-1/3 cups flour and the salt. Cut In margarine until mixture resembles coarse meal. Add milk, stirring until entire mixture is moistened. Pat half the dough in bottom and about half way up the sides of greased 9 x 9 x 2-inch baking pan. Set aside.

- Stir together the 2 tablespoons flour, the cinnamon, nutmeg and sugar. Mix with sliced apples. Spoon into crust. Sprinkle with lemon juice. Set aside.

- Roll out remaining dough on lightly floured surface to fit pan. Place over apples. Prick crust with fork 3 or 4 times.

- Bake in oven at 375° F. about 45 minutes or until apples are tender. While still warm, drizzle with *Confectioners' Sugar Glaze.* Cut into squares and serve warm or cooled.

Yield:  9 servings

VARIATION:

2 cups Corn Flakes cereal, crushed to measure 1/2 cup, may be substituted for the Rice Krispies cereal.

# confectioners' sugar glaze

**1 cup sifted confectioners' sugar**
**4 teaspoons warm water**

- Combine sugar and water in small mixing bowl, stirring until smooth. If a thinner glaze is desired, add 1/2 to 1 teaspoon more water.

Yield:   1/3 cup

VARIATIONS:

4 teaspoons lemon or orange juice may be substituted for the water.

# caramel crunch topping

**1/2 cup regular margarine or butter**
**1-1/4 cups Corn Flake Crumbs**
**3/4 cup firmly packed brown sugar**
**3/4 cup shredded coconut**
**1/2 cup coarsely chopped nuts**
**1/4 cup regular all-purpose flour**
**1/4 teaspoon ground cinnamon**
**1/4 teaspoon ground nutmeg**

- Melt margarine in medium-size saucepan. Remove from heat. Add remaining ingredients. Stir until well combined. Spread mixture evenly on ungreased baking sheet.
- Bake in oven at 350° F. about 12 minutes or until lightly browned and slightly crisp. Stir once or twice as mixture bakes. Cool completely. Serve over ice cream or pudding.

Yield:   4 cups

NOTE:   Topping becomes more crisp as it cools. Extra topping may be stored in refrigerator in tightly covered container.

# ice cream party pie

1/3 cup peanut butter
1/3 cup corn syrup
2 cups Rice Krispies cereal
1/2 cup strawberry jam or preserves
1 quart strawberry ice cream, slightly softened

● Measure peanut butter and corn syrup into medium-size mixing bowl. Stir until thoroughly combined. Add Rice Krispies cereal. Mix until well coated. With back of spoon, press mixture evenly around sides and in bottom of 9-inch pie pan to form crust. Chill until firm.

● Spread 1/4 cup of the jam over chilled crust. Spoon softened ice cream over jam. Freeze until firm. Swirl the remaining 1/4 cup jam over top of frozen pie.

Yield:   one 9-inch pie

NOTE:   To cut pie easily, place hot wet towel under bottom and around sides of pan. Allow to stand a few minutes.

VARIATION:

Vanilla or chocolate ice cream may be substituted for the strawberry ice cream.

# ambrosia pie

1-3/4 cups cold water
1 package (4-3/4 oz.) cherry-plum flavor Junket Danish Dessert
1/2 cup mandarin orange segments, well drained
1 can (8-1/4 oz.) crushed pineapple, well drained
1-1/2 cups sliced bananas
1 baked 9-inch pie crust (see pages 138, 139 and 197)
Whipped topping
2 tablespoons toasted flaked coconut

152

- Measure cold water into medium-size saucepan. Stir in Danish Dessert. Bring to full boil over medium heat. Boil 1 minute, stirring constantly. Remove from heat. Cool completely.

- Fold orange segments, pineapple and bananas into cooled Danish Dessert. Spoon into baked pie crust. Chill 3 to 4 hours or until firm. At serving time, garnish with whipped topping and toasted coconut.

Yield:   one 9-inch pie

# key lime pie

**1/2 pint (1 cup) whipping cream**

**2 tablespoons sifted confectioners' sugar**

**3 egg yolks**

**1 can (15 oz.) sweetened condensed milk**

**1/2 cup fresh lime juice (about 5 limes) or bottled lime juice**

**1 drop green food coloring (optional)**

**3/4 teaspoon grated lime peel (optional)**

**1 baked 9-inch pie crust (see pages 138, 139 and 197)**

**Lime slices**

- Whip cream with sugar until stiff peaks form. Chill.

- In medium-size mixing bowl, beat egg yolks until well blended. Stir in milk. Add lime juice gradually, stirring constantly. Stir in food coloring and lime peel. Fold in 1 cup of the whipped cream.

- Pour filling into baked pie crust. Chill until firm, about 2 hours. Just before serving, top with remaining whipped cream and garnish with lime slices.

Yield:   one 9-inch pie

# kwik krazy kake

1-1/2 cups regular all-purpose flour
1 teaspoon baking soda
1/2 teaspoon salt
1 teaspoon ground cinnamon
1 cup sugar
1/4 cup unsweetened cocoa
1/2 cup All-Bran cereal or Bran Buds cereal
1 cup cold strong coffee
1/4 cup vegetable oil
1 tablespoon vinegar
1 teaspoon vanilla flavoring

- Stir together flour, soda, salt, cinnamon, sugar and cocoa. Set aside.

- Measure All-Bran cereal and coffee into ungreased 8 x 8 x 2-inch baking pan. Stir to combine. Let stand 1 to 2 minutes or until cereal is softened. Stir in oil, vinegar and vanilla. Add flour mixture, stirring until smooth.

- Bake in oven at 350° F. about 40 minutes or until wooden pick inserted near center comes out clean. Cool completely. Cut into squares and serve with whipped topping, if desired.

Yield:  9 servings

VARIATION:

1 cup 40% Bran Flakes cereal may be substituted for the All-Bran cereal.

# Danish dessert cake

1 package (18-1/2 oz.) yellow or white cake mix
3 eggs
1/2 cup vegetable oil
1 cup water
1 package (4-3/4 oz.) Junket Danish Dessert, any flavor
Confectioners' Sugar Glaze (see page 151)

- Place all ingredients in large bowl of electric mixer. Stir to combine. Beat at medium speed for 3 minutes. Pour into well-greased and floured 10 x 4-inch tube pan.

- Bake in oven at 350° F. about 45 minutes or until wooden pick inserted near center comes out clean. Remove from oven. Cool 10 minutes before removing from pan. Invert onto serving plate. Drizzle with *Confectioners' Sugar Glaze.*

Yield:  16 servings

# COOKIES

2

# COOKIES

There's no doubt about it . . . cookies are enjoyed around the world. From the cookie jar favorites that always need replenishing to the once-a-year specialties, cookies of all shapes, sizes and flavors make a tempting treat for cookie-lovers everywhere.

1.  frosted raisin bars, p. 168
2.  choco-banana bars, p. 160
3.  cinnamon balls, p. 171
4.  carnival cookies, p. 162
5.  tiger cookies, p. 176

6.  marshmallow treats, p. 159
7.  cherry winks, p. 166
8.  chocolate wafer stack-ups, p. 175
9.  corn flakes macaroons, p. 166

# marshmallow treats

**1/4 cup regular margarine or butter**
**1 package (10 oz., about 40) regular marshmallows**
**or 4 cups miniature marshmallows**
**5 cups Rice Krispies cereal**

- Melt margarine in large saucepan over low heat. Add marshmallows and stir until completely melted. Cook over low heat 3 minutes longer, stirring constantly. Remove from heat.

- Add Rice Krispies cereal. Stir until well coated.

- Using buttered spatula or waxed paper, press mixture evenly into buttered 13 x 9 x 2-inch pan. Cut into 2-inch squares when cool.

Yield:   24 squares, 2 x 2 inches

NOTE:   Best results are obtained when using fresh marshmallows.

## VARIATIONS:

**To make thicker squares:**   Press warm mixture into buttered 9 x 9 x 2-inch pan.

**Marshmallow Creme Treats:**   About 2 cups marshmallow creme may be substituted for marshmallows. Add to melted margarine and stir until well blended. Cook over low heat about 5 minutes longer, stirring constantly. Remove from heat. Proceed as directed in step 2 above.

**Peanut Treats:**   Add 1 cup salted cocktail peanuts with the cereal.

**Peanut Butter Treats:**   Stir 1/4 cup peanut butter into marshmallow mixture just before adding the cereal.

**Raisin Treats:**   Add 1 cup seedless raisins with the cereal.

**Cocoa Krispies Cereal Treats:**   6 cups Cocoa Krispies cereal may be substituted for the 5 cups Rice Krispies cereal.

See page 198 for microwave directions.

159

# choco-banana bars

1 cup regular all-purpose flour
1/2 teaspoon baking powder
1/4 teaspoon baking soda
1 teaspoon salt
1/2 teaspoon ground cinnamon
1/4 cup regular margarine or butter, softened
3/4 cup sugar
1 cup mashed, fully ripe bananas (about 3 medium-size)
1 egg
1/4 cup milk
1 cup All-Bran cereal or Bran Buds cereal
1 package (6 oz., 1 cup) semi-sweet chocolate morsels, melted
1 cup chopped nuts

- Stir together flour, baking powder, soda, salt and cinnamon. Set aside.

- Measure margarine, sugar, bananas, egg, milk, All-Bran cereal and melted chocolate into large mixing bowl. Beat until well combined. Add flour mixture. Mix well. Stir in nuts. Spread batter evenly in greased and floured 13 x 9 x 2-inch baking pan.

- Bake in oven at 350° F. about 30 minutes or until wooden pick inserted near center comes out clean. Cool completely. Spread with *Chocolate Velvet Frosting.* Cut into bars.

Yield:   32 bars, 1-1/2 x 2 inches

# chocolate velvet frosting

2 tablespoons shortening
1 package (6 oz., 1 cup) semi-sweet chocolate morsels
1 cup sifted confectioners' sugar
1/4 cup milk
1/8 teaspoon salt
1/4 teaspoon vanilla flavoring

Melt shortening and chocolate together in medium-size saucepan over very low heat, stirring constantly until smooth. Remove from heat. Add remaining ingredients, mixing until smooth.

## crunchy peanut butter cookies

2 cups regular all-purpose flour

2 teaspoons baking soda

1/4 teaspoon salt

1 cup regular margarine or butter, softened

1 cup peanut butter

3/4 cup granulated sugar

3/4 cup firmly packed brown sugar

2 eggs

1 teaspoon vanilla flavoring

20 Frosted Mini-Wheats biscuits or Toasted Mini-Wheats biscuits, crushed to fine shreds

Stir together flour, soda and salt. Set aside.

In large mixing bowl, beat margarine, peanut butter, granulated sugar and brown sugar until light and fluffy. Add eggs and vanilla. Beat well. Add flour mixture and crushed Frosted Mini-Wheats biscuits. Mix until well combined.

Drop by level measuring-tablespoon onto ungreased baking sheets. Using back of fork, flatten each cookie in crisscross pattern.

Bake in oven at 350° F. about 14 minutes or until lightly browned. Remove immediately from baking sheets. Cool on wire racks.

Yield:  about 5-1/2 dozen

VARIATION:

3 cups Product 19 multivitamin and iron supplement cereal, crushed to measure 1-1/2 cups, may be substituted for the Frosted Mini-Wheats biscuits.

# carnival cookies

2 cups regular all-purpose flour
1/2 teaspoon baking powder
1/4 teaspoon salt
1/2 cup shortening
1/2 cup regular margarine or butter, softened
1/2 cup sugar
2 eggs
1/2 cup orange juice
2 cups Froot Loops cereal, crushed to fine crumbs

- Stir together flour, baking powder and salt. Set aside.

- In large mixing bowl, beat shortening, margarine and sugar until light and fluffy. Add eggs and orange juice. Beat well. Add flour mixture. Mix until well combined. Stir in crushed Froot Loops cereal. Drop by level measuring-tablespoon onto ungreased baking sheets.

- Bake in oven at 350° F. about 12 minutes or until lightly browned. Remove immediately from baking sheets. Cool on wire racks. When completely cooled, frost with *Orange Icing.* Decorate with additional cereal, whole or crushed, if desired.

Yield:  about 4 dozen

# orange icing

2 cups sifted confectioners' sugar
3 tablespoons regular margarine or butter, softened
2 tablespoons orange juice

- Measure sugar, margarine and orange juice into small mixing bowl. Beat until smooth.

# chocolate chip cookies

**2-1/4 cups regular all-purpose flour**
**1 teaspoon baking soda**
**1/2 teaspoon salt**
**1 cup regular margarine or butter, softened**
**3/4 cup granulated sugar**
**3/4 cup firmly packed brown sugar**
**2 eggs**
**1 teaspoon vanilla flavoring**
**2 cups Rice Krispies cereal**
**1 package (6 oz., 1 cup) semi-sweet chocolate morsels**

- Stir together flour, soda and salt. Set aside.

- In large mixing bowl, beat margarine, granulated sugar and brown sugar until well combined. Add eggs and vanilla. Beat well. Add flour mixture. Mix thoroughly. Stir in Rice Krispies cereal and chocolate morsels. Drop by level measuring-tablespoon onto greased baking sheets.

- Bake in oven at 350° F. about 10 minutes or until lightly browned. Let cool about 1 minute before removing from baking sheets. Place on wire racks.

Yield: about 5 dozen

## VARIATIONS:

**Peanut Butter Cookies:** Mix 3/4 cup peanut butter into margarine-sugar mixture.

**Chocolate Chip Raisin Cookies:** Add 1 cup seedless raisins with the chocolate morsels.

**Holiday Fruit Cookies:** In place of chocolate morsels, use 1 cup finely cut, mixed candied fruit.

**Chocolate Chip Bran Cookies:** 1 cup All-Bran cereal or Bran Buds cereal may be substituted for the Rice Krispies cereal.

# fudge sandwich surprises

**1/4 cup regular margarine or butter**
**1 package (10 oz., about 40) regular marshmallows**
**or 4 cups miniature marshmallows**
**1/4 cup peanut butter**
**5 cups Rice Krispies cereal**

      \*      \*      \*      \*      \*

**1/4 cup regular margarine or butter, softened**
**3 tablespoons hot water**
**1 package (10-1/2 oz.) Salada 4 Minute Fudge Mix**

- Melt 1/4 cup margarine in large saucepan over low heat. Add marshmallows and stir until completely melted. Cook over low heat 3 minutes longer, stirring constantly. Stir in peanut butter. Remove from heat. Add Rice Krispies cereal. Stir until well coated.

- Using buttered spatula or waxed paper, press mixture evenly into buttered 15-1/2 x 10-1/2 x 1-inch pan. Chill about 20 minutes or until firm.

- Measure remaining 1/4 cup margarine and the water into small bowl of electric mixer. Add Fudge Mix, mixing until well combined. Beat on high speed of electric mixer for 2 minutes.

- Cut cereal mixture in half crosswise. Spread Fudge mixture over one half. Top with other half of cereal mixture, gently pressing halves together. Chill until firm. Cut into 1-inch squares.

Yield:   80 squares, 1 x 1 inch

NOTE:   May be stored in refrigerator or at room temperature.

# date nut balls

**1/2 cup regular margarine or butter**
**1-1/2 cups cut, pitted dates**
**1/3 cup chopped maraschino cherries**
**3/4 cup sugar**
**3 cups Special K cereal**
**1 cup chopped nuts**

- Measure margarine, dates, cherries and sugar into medium-size saucepan. Cook over medium heat, stirring constantly, until mixture becomes a soft paste. Remove from heat. Add Special K cereal and nuts. Mix thoroughly.

- Portion by level measuring-tablespoon onto waxed paper or buttered baking sheet. Shape into balls. Let stand until cool.

Yield:   about 3-1/2 dozen

# Kriss Kringle wreath

**1/3 cup regular margarine or butter**
**1 package (10 oz., about 40) regular marshmallows**
**or 4 cups miniature marshmallows**
**1/2 teaspoon vanilla flavoring (optional)**
**1 teaspoon green food coloring**
**6 cups Corn Flakes cereal**
**Red cinnamon candies**

- Melt margarine in large saucepan. Add marshmallows and cook over low heat, stirring constantly, until marshmallows melt and mixture is syrupy. Remove from heat. Stir in vanilla and green food coloring.

- Add Corn Flakes cereal. Stir until well coated.

- Press warm marshmallow mixture into buttered 6-cup ring mold or shape into ring on serving plate. Remove from mold and dot with red candies. Slice to serve.

Yield:   about 30 one-inch slices

VARIATION:

With buttered fingers, shape warm mixture into individual wreaths, using 1/3 cup for each. Dot with red cinnamon candies. Yield:   1 dozen.

# cherry winks

2-1/4 cups regular all-purpose flour
2 teaspoons baking powder
1/2 teaspoon salt
3/4 cup regular margarine or butter, softened
1 cup sugar
2 eggs
2 tablespoons milk
1 teaspoon vanilla flavoring
1 cup chopped nuts
1 cup finely cut, pitted dates
1/3 cup finely chopped maraschino cherries
2-2/3 cups Corn Flakes cereal, crushed to measure 1-1/3 cups
15 maraschino cherries, cut into quarters

- Stir together flour, baking powder and salt. Set aside.

- In large mixing bowl, beat margarine and sugar until light and fluffy. Add eggs. Beat well. Stir in milk and vanilla. Add flour mixture. Mix until well combined. Stir in nuts, dates and chopped cherries.

- Portion dough using level measuring-tablespoon. Shape into balls. Roll in crushed Corn Flakes cereal. Place about 2 inches apart on greased baking sheets. Top each with cherry quarter.

- Bake in oven at 375° F. about 10 minutes or until lightly browned. Remove immediately from baking sheets. Cool on wire racks.

Yield:   about 5 dozen

# corn flakes macaroons

4 egg whites
1/4 teaspoon cream of tartar
1 teaspoon vanilla flavoring
1-1/3 cups sugar
1 cup chopped pecans
1 cup shredded coconut
3 cups Corn Flakes cereal

- In large mixing bowl, beat egg whites until foamy. Stir in cream of tartar and vanilla. Gradually add sugar, beating until stiff and glossy. Fold in pecans, coconut and Corn Flakes cereal. Drop by rounded measuring-tablespoon onto well-greased baking sheets.

- Bake in oven at 325° F. about 20 minutes or until lightly browned. Remove immediately from baking sheets. Cool on wire racks.

Yield: about 3 dozen

VARIATION

Merry Macaroons: Fold in 1/2 cup crushed peppermint candy with pecans and coconut.

# chewy orange crisps

2 cups regular all-purpose flour
1/4 teaspoon baking soda
1/2 teaspoon salt
1 cup regular margarine or butter, softened
1 cup granulated sugar
1/2 cup firmly packed brown sugar
1 teaspoon grated orange peel
2 eggs
2 cups Raisin Bran cereal

- Stir together flour, soda and salt. Set aside.

- In large mixing bowl, beat margarine, granulated sugar, brown sugar and orange peel until well combined. Add eggs. Beat well. Add flour mixture. Mix thoroughly. Stir in Raisin Bran cereal. Drop by level measuring-tablespoon onto ungreased baking sheets.

- Bake in oven at 350° F. about 15 minutes or until golden brown. Cool slightly before removing from baking sheets. Place on wire racks.

Yield: about 4 dozen

# frosted raisin bars

1 cup regular all-purpose flour
1 teaspoon baking powder
1/2 teaspoon salt
1/2 cup regular margarine or butter, softened
1/2 cup granulated sugar
1/2 cup firmly packed brown sugar
2 eggs
1 teaspoon vanilla flavoring
3/4 cup All-Bran cereal or Bran Buds cereal
3/4 cup seedless raisins

- Stir together flour, baking powder and salt. Set aside.

- In large mixing bowl, beat margarine, granulated sugar and brown sugar until light and fluffy. Add eggs and vanilla. Beat well. Stir in All-Bran cereal and raisins. Add flour mixture, mixing until well combined. Spread batter evenly in greased 9 x 9 x 2-inch baking pan.

- Bake in oven at 350° F. about 35 minutes or until wooden pick inserted near center comes out clean. Cool completely. Spread with *Confectioners' Sugar Frosting.*

Yield:   18 bars, 1-1/2 x 3 inches

# confectioners' sugar frosting

2 cups sifted confectioners' sugar
2 tablespoons regular margarine or butter, softened
2 tablespoons milk
1/2 teaspoon vanilla flavoring

- Measure all ingredients into small mixing bowl. Beat until smooth.

1 cup regular all-purpose flour

1 teaspoon baking powder

1/4 teaspoon baking soda

1 teaspoon salt

1 teaspoon ground cinnamon

1/2 teaspoon ground nutmeg

15 Frosted Mini-Wheats biscuits or Toasted Mini-Wheats biscuits,
   crushed to measure 1-1/3 cups

1/4 cup milk

1 cup pumpkin

1 teaspoon vanilla flavoring

1/2 cup shortening

1/2 cup firmly packed brown sugar

1 egg

*          *          *          *          *

1 egg

1/4 cup firmly packed brown sugar

1 cup flaked coconut

1/2 cup chopped walnuts

- Stir together flour, baking powder, soda, salt, cinnamon and nutmeg. Set aside.

- In medium-size mixing bowl, stir together crushed Frosted Mini-Wheats biscuits, milk, pumpkin and vanilla. Let stand 15 minutes.

- Meanwhile, in large mixing bowl, beat shortening and the 1/2 cup sugar until light and fluffy. Add 1 egg. Beat well. Stir in pumpkin mixture. Add flour mixture, mixing until well combined. Spread batter evenly in greased 13 x 9 x 2-inch baking pan.

- In small mixing bowl, beat the remaining egg until thick and lemon colored. Gradually add the 1/4 cup sugar, beating until thick. Stir in coconut and walnuts. Spread evenly over batter in pan.

- Bake in oven at 350° F. about 30 minutes or until wooden pick inserted near center comes out clean. Serve plain or with ice cream or whipped topping.

Yield:  18 bars, 2 x 3 inches

# magic cookie bars

1-1/2 cups Corn Flake Crumbs

3 tablespoons sugar

1/2 cup regular margarine or butter, softened

1 cup coarsely chopped walnuts

1 package (6 oz., 1 cup) semi-sweet chocolate morsels

1 can (3-1/2 oz., 1-1/3 cups) flaked coconut

1 can (15 oz.) sweetened condensed milk

● Measure Corn Flake Crumbs, sugar and margarine into 13 x 9 x 2-inch baking pan. Mix thoroughly. With back of spoon, press mixture evenly and firmly in bottom of pan to form crust.

● Sprinkle walnuts, chocolate morsels and coconut evenly over Crumbs crust. Pour sweetened condensed milk evenly over top.

● Bake in oven at 350° F. about 25 minutes or until lightly browned around edges. Cool completely before cutting into bars.

Yield:   48 bars, 1 x 2 inches

See page 194 for microwave directions.

# fruit crisps

1-3/4 cups regular all-purpose flour

1/2 teaspoon baking soda

1/2 teaspoon salt

2 cups Product 19 multivitamin and iron supplement cereal, crushed to measure 1 cup

1 cup regular margarine or butter, softened

1 cup granulated sugar

1/2 cup firmly packed brown sugar

1 egg

1 teaspoon vanilla flavoring

1 cup finely cut, mixed candied fruit

- Stir together flour, soda, salt and crushed Product 19 supplement cereal. Set aside.

- In large mixing bowl, beat margarine, granulated sugar and brown sugar until well combined. Add egg and vanilla. Beat well. Add flour mixture. Mix thoroughly. Stir in mixed candied fruit. Drop by level measuring-table-spoon onto ungreased baking sheets.

- Bake in oven at 350° F. about 12 minutes or until golden brown. Cool slightly before removing from baking sheets. Place on wire racks.

Yield:   about 4-1/2 dozen

# cinnamon balls

**1-3/4 cups regular all-purpose flour**
**1 teaspoon ground cinnamon**
**3/4 cup Corn Flake Crumbs**
**1 cup regular margarine or butter, softened**
**1/3 cup granulated sugar**
**2 teaspoons vanilla flavoring**
**1 cup finely chopped nuts**
**1 cup sifted confectioners' sugar**

- Stir together flour, cinnamon and Corn Flake Crumbs. Set aside.

- In large mixing bowl, beat margarine and granulated sugar until well combined. Stir in vanilla. Add Crumbs mixture. Mix well. Stir in nuts. Portion dough using level measuring-tablespoon. Shape into balls. Place on greased baking sheets.

- Bake in oven at 350° F. about 20 minutes or until lightly browned. Remove from baking sheets. While still warm, roll in confectioners' sugar. Cool on wire racks.

Yield:   about 3 dozen

**1-1/4 cups regular all-purpose flour**
**1/2 teaspoon baking soda**
**1/2 teaspoon ground cinnamon**
**1/4 teaspoon ground nutmeg**
**1/4 teaspoon ground ginger**
**2 cups 40% Bran Flakes cereal**
**1/2 cup milk**
**1/2 cup regular margarine or butter, softened**
**1 cup firmly packed brown sugar**
**2 eggs**
**1 teaspoon vanilla flavoring**
**1/2 cup coarsely chopped peanuts**
**1 cup seedless raisins**

- Stir together flour, soda, cinnamon, nutmeg and ginger. Set aside.

- Measure 40% Bran Flakes cereal and milk into small mixing bowl. Stir to combine. Let stand 1 to 2 minutes or until cereal is softened.

- In large mixing bowl, beat margarine and sugar until light and fluffy. Add eggs, vanilla and cereal mixture. Beat well. Add flour mixture. Mix until well combined. Stir in peanuts and raisins. Drop by level measuring-tablespoon onto lightly greased baking sheets.

- Bake in oven at 375° F. about 11 minutes or until lightly browned. Remove immediately from baking sheets. Cool on wire racks. When completely cooled, frost with *Vanilla Icing*. Sprinkle with additional chopped peanuts, if desired.

Yield:  about 4 dozen

# vanilla icing

**1-1/2 cups sifted confectioners' sugar**
**2 tablespoons regular margarine or butter, softened**
**5 teaspoons milk**
**1 teaspoon vanilla flavoring**

- Measure all ingredients into small mixing bowl. Beat until smooth.

1/2 cup regular margarine or butter, softened

1/4 cup granulated sugar

2/3 cup regular all-purpose flour

2/3 cup All-Bran cereal or Bran Buds cereal

*       *       *       *       *

2/3 cup finely cut, dried apricots

1/2 cup regular all-purpose flour

1/2 teaspoon baking powder

1/4 teaspoon salt

1 cup firmly packed brown sugar

2 eggs

1/2 teaspoon vanilla flavoring

1/2 cup finely chopped nuts

Confectioners' sugar

- For crust, measure margarine, granulated sugar and the 2/3 cup flour into small mixing bowl. Beat until smooth. Mix in All-Bran cereal. Spread mixture evenly in bottom of greased 8 x 8 x 2-inch baking pan.

- Bake in oven at 350° F. about 25 minutes or until lightly browned. Remove from oven. Cool slightly.

- While crust is baking, rinse apricots. Place in small mixing bowl. Cover with very hot water. Let stand about 10 minutes or until tender. Drain well. Set aside.

- Stir together the remaining 1/2 cup flour, the baking powder and salt. Set aside.

- Place brown sugar, eggs and vanilla in large mixing bowl. Beat well. Add flour mixture. Mix well. Stir in nuts and apricots. Spread mixture over baked crust.

- Return to oven and bake about 45 minutes longer or until lightly browned. Cool. Sprinkle with confectioners' sugar.

Yield:   32 bars, 1 x 2 inches

# walnut drop cookies

1-1/2 cups regular all-purpose flour
1/2 teaspoon baking soda
1 teaspoon salt
1 cup regular margarine or butter, softened
1 cup granulated sugar
1/2 cup firmly packed brown sugar
1 egg
1 teaspoon vanilla flavoring
1 cup chopped walnuts
2 cups Product 19 multivitamin and iron supplement cereal, crushed to measure 1 cup

- Stir together flour, soda and salt. Set aside.

- In large mixing bowl, beat margarine, granulated sugar and brown sugar until light and fluffy. Add egg and vanilla. Beat well. Add flour mixture. Mix until well combined. Stir in walnuts and crushed Product 19 supplement cereal. Drop by level measuring-tablespoon onto ungreased baking sheets.

- Bake in oven at 350° F. about 14 minutes or until golden brown. Cool slightly before removing from baking sheets. Place on wire racks.

Yield:   about 5 dozen

# scotch treats

1 package (6 oz., 1 cup) butterscotch morsels
1/2 cup peanut butter
3 cups Rice Krispies cereal

- Melt butterscotch morsels and peanut butter together in large saucepan over very low heat, stirring constantly until smooth. Remove from heat. Add Rice Krispies cereal. Stir until well coated.

- Press mixture evenly into buttered 9 x 9 x 2-inch pan. Chill until firm. Cut into 1-1/2-inch squares.

Yield:   36 squares, 1-1/2 x 1-1/2 inches

**VARIATIONS:**

**Coconut Scotch Treats:**   Add 1 cup flaked coconut with the cereal.

**Marshmallow Scotch Treats:**   Add 1/2 cup miniature marshmallows with the cereal.

**Peanut Scotch Treats:**   Add 1 cup salted peanuts with the cereal.

**Raisin Scotch Treats:**   Add 1 cup seedless raisins with the cereal.

# chocolate wafer stack-ups

**1-1/2 cups regular all-purpose flour**
  **3/4 teaspoon salt**
  **1/2 cup regular margarine or butter, softened**
    **1 cup sugar**
    **1 egg**
    **1 teaspoon vanilla flavoring**
    **2 squares (1 oz. each) unsweetened chocolate, melted**
    **2 cups Rice Krispies cereal, crushed to measure 1 cup**
  **3/4 cup coarsely chopped nuts**

- Stir together flour and salt. Set aside.
- In large mixing bowl, beat margarine and sugar until light and fluffy. Add egg, vanilla and melted chocolate. Mix well. Add flour mixture. Mix until well combined. Stir in crushed Rice Krispies cereal and nuts. Drop by rounded measuring-teaspoon onto lightly greased baking sheets. Using bottom of glass, press dough into flat rounds.
- Bake in oven at 325° F. about 10 minutes or until set. Cool slightly before removing from baking sheets. Place on wire racks.
- Spread half the cookies with *Vanilla Icing* (see page 172). Top with remaining cookies. Spread top cookies with *Icing.* Sprinkle with additional chopped nuts, if desired.

Yield:   about 3 dozen

1-3/4 cups regular all-purpose flour

1/2 teaspoon baking soda

1/2 teaspoon salt

1 cup regular margarine or butter, softened

1 cup sugar

2 eggs

1 teaspoon vanilla flavoring

3 cups Sugar Frosted Flakes of Corn cereal, crushed to measure
1-1/2 cups

1 package (6 oz., 1 cup) semi-sweet chocolate morsels, melted

Stir together flour, soda and salt. Set aside.

In large mixing bowl, beat margarine and sugar until light and fluffy. Add eggs and vanilla. Beat well. Add flour mixture, mixing until well combined. Stir in crushed Sugar Frosted Flakes of Corn cereal. Drizzle melted chocolate over dough. With knife, swirl melted chocolate gently through dough to achieve marbled appearance. Drop by rounded measuring-tablespoon onto ungreased baking sheets.

Bake in oven at 350° F. about 12 minutes or until lightly browned. Remove immediately from baking sheets. Cool on wire racks.

Yield: about 5 dozen

1-1/2 cups regular all-purpose flour

1/2 teaspoon baking soda

1/2 teaspoon salt

1 cup regular margarine or butter, softened

1 cup granulated sugar

1/2 cup firmly packed brown sugar

1 egg

1 teaspoon vanilla flavoring

2 cups Cocoa Krispies cereal

1 package (6 oz., 1 cup) butterscotch morsels

- Stir together flour, soda and salt. Set aside.

- In large mixing bowl, beat margarine, granulated sugar and brown sugar until light and fluffy. Add egg and vanilla. Beat well. Add flour mixture. Mix until well combined. Stir in Cocoa Krispies cereal and butterscotch morsels. Drop by level measuring-tablespoon onto ungreased baking sheets.

- Bake in oven at 350° F. about 14 minutes or until golden brown. Cool slightly before removing from baking sheets. Place on wire racks.

Yield:    about 5 dozen


# saucepan brownies

---

**3/4 cup regular all-purpose flour**

**1/4 teaspoon baking soda**

**1/4 teaspoon salt**

**1/2 cup sugar**

**1/3 cup vegetable oil**

   **2 tablespoons water**

   **1 package (6 oz., 1 cup) semi-sweet chocolate morsels**

   **1 teaspoon vanilla flavoring**

   **2 eggs**

**1/2 cup All-Bran cereal or Bran Buds cereal**

**3/4 cup coarsely chopped nuts**


- Stir together flour, soda and salt. Set aside.

- Combine sugar, oil and water in large saucepan. Bring to boil, stirring frequently. Remove from heat. Add chocolate morsels and vanilla, stirring until chocolate is melted. Add eggs. Beat well.

- Add flour mixture, mixing until well combined. Stir in All-Bran cereal and nuts. Spread batter evenly in greased 8 x 8 x 2-inch baking pan.

- Bake in oven at 325° F. about 30 minutes or until wooden pick inserted near center comes out clean. Cool completely before cutting into squares.

Yield:    16 squares, 2 x 2 inches

# peanut butter clusters

**1 package (6 oz., 1 cup) butterscotch morsels**
**1/4 cup peanut butter**
**3 cups Product 19 multivitamin and iron supplement cereal**

- Melt butterscotch morsels and peanut butter together in medium-size saucepan over very low heat, stirring constantly until smooth. Remove from heat. Add Product 19 supplement cereal. Stir until well coated.

- Drop by level measuring-tablespoon onto buttered baking sheet. Chill until firm.

Yield:   about 2 dozen

See page 193 for microwave directions.

# Special K cookies

**3 cups Special K cereal, crushed to measure 2 cups**
**1 cup regular all-purpose flour**
**1 teaspoon baking powder**
**1/4 teaspoon salt**
**1/2 cup regular margarine or butter, softened**
**2/3 cup sugar**
**1 egg**
**1 teaspoon vanilla flavoring**

- Stir together 1 cup of the crushed Special K cereal, the flour, baking powder and salt. Set aside.

- In large mixing bowl, beat margarine and sugar until light and fluffy. Add egg and vanilla. Beat well. Add flour mixture. Mix until well combined. Portion dough using level measuring-tablespoon. Shape into balls. Roll in the remaining 1 cup crushed cereal. Place about 2 inches apart on ungreased baking sheets.

- Bake in oven at 375° F. about 12 minutes or until lightly browned. Remove immediately from baking sheets. Cool on wire racks.

Yield:   about 2-1/2 dozen

# chocolate snowcaps

1-1/2 cups regular all-purpose flour

2 teaspoons baking powder

1 teaspoon salt

1/4 cup shortening

4 squares (1 oz. each) unsweetened chocolate

2 cups granulated sugar

4 eggs

1 teaspoon vanilla flavoring

1 cup All-Bran cereal or Bran Buds cereal

3/4 cup chopped nuts

1/2 cup sifted confectioners' sugar

- Stir together flour, baking powder and salt. Set aside.

- Melt shortening and chocolate together in large saucepan over very low heat, stirring constantly until smooth. Remove from heat. Cool. Stir in sugar. Add eggs, one at a time, beating well after each addition. Stir in vanilla. Add flour mixture, mixing until well combined. Stir in All-Bran cereal and nuts. Chill until dough is stiff.

- Portion dough using level measuring-tablespoon. Shape into balls. Roll in confectioners' sugar. Place about 2 inches apart on greased baking sheets.

- Bake in oven at 350° F. about 15 minutes or until set. Cool slightly before removing from baking sheets. Place on wire racks.

Yield:   about 5 dozen

NOTE:   Cookies are soft when removed from oven, but will become firm when cool.

MICROWAVE

# MICROWAVE

Cooking with microwave energy is becoming more and more popular due to its speed and energy-saving advantages. You'll soon discover that Kellogg products are as versatile in this ultramodern method of cooking as they are in conventional cookery. And most ready-to-eat cereals add a golden brown touch that makes many foods more attractive.

The next few pages contain a variety of delicious recipes that have been adapted for the microwave oven. When comparing a recipe with its conventionally prepared counterpart, there will often be some differences in the lists of ingredients. Also, slight differences in the final textures and appearances are to be expected.

Here are a few tips to help you better understand the microwave cooking techniques used in the Kellogg Company Test Center.

**We wish you many rewarding new experiences as together we explore the futuristic world of microwave cooking—today!**

1. Mexican stuffed peppers, p. 186
2. marshmallow treats, p. 198
3. meat 'n tater pie, p. 187
4. Danish dessert, p. 192
5. French cherry dessert, p. 199
6. magic cookie bars, p. 194
7. peanut butter clusters, p. 193
8. crunchy party snack, p. 198
9. herbed zucchini bake, p. 192
10. molasses brown bread, p. 184

## power settings

A FULL POWER (maximum output) setting is used in all recipes to minimize differences among the many brands of ovens. The microwave units used in our Test Center had FULL POWER outputs of 650 watts and 675 watts of power. If the FULL POWER wattage of your microwave oven is not 650 or 675 watts, be sure to adjust cooking times accordingly: decrease cooking time if your oven has more than 675 watts, and increase time if your oven has less power than 650 watts.

## cookware

Various sizes of glass cookware commonly on hand are called for in the Kellogg microwave recipes. Plastic and paper containers can also be used. Do not use metal cookware in the microwave oven. Refer to your unit's instruction manual for further cookware information and precautions.

## rotation and stirring

To assure more evenly cooked foods, rotation or stirring is sometimes necessary. When several items such as food in custard cups or individual quick breads are being cooked together, they should be placed in a circle and rotated occasionally. Individual items may need to be removed at different times since they often cook at varying rates.

Some recipes indicate a standing period after removal from the oven, permitting heat to be conducted evenly throughout the food. This completes the required cooking.

## covering foods

Plastic wrap or waxed paper is needed to cover many dishes during cooking. The purpose of the covering is to retain moisture and help eliminate splattering. Be sure to poke holes in the covering before cooking to allow steam to escape. Do not use foil to cover foods.

## temperature testing

By checking the internal temperature of some meat or poultry dishes you can be certain that the product is thoroughly cooked. Use only a microwave oven thermometer if testing the product while cooking in the microwave unit. A regular meat thermometer may be used once the food has been removed from the oven.

### precautions to avoid possible exposure to excessive microwave energy

(a) Do not attempt to operate your microwave oven with the door open since open-door operation can result in harmful exposure to microwave energy. It is important not to defeat or tamper with the safety interlocks.

(b) Do not place any object between the oven front face and the door or allow soil or cleaner residue to accumulate on sealing surfaces.

(c) Do not operate the oven if it is damaged. It is particularly important that the oven door close properly and that there is no damage to the: (1) door (bent), (2) hinges and latches (broken or loosened), (3) door seals and sealing surfaces.

(d) The oven should not be adjusted or repaired by anyone except properly qualified service personnel.

# molasses brown bread

1 cup regular all-purpose flour
1 teaspoon baking soda
1/2 teaspoon salt
1/2 teaspoon ground cinnamon
1 egg
1 cup All-Bran cereal or Bran Buds cereal
1/2 cup seedless raisins
2 tablespoons shortening
1/3 cup molasses
3/4 cup very hot water

- Stir together flour, soda, salt and cinnamon. Set aside.
- In large mixing bowl, beat egg slightly. Mix in All-Bran cereal, raisins, shortening and molasses. Add water, stirring until shortening is melted. Add flour mixture, stirring only until combined. Portion batter evenly into six 6-ounce foam or paper hot drink cups. Place in circle in microwave oven.
- Microwave on full power 4 minutes, rotating every minute. Remove each loaf when wooden pick inserted near center comes out clean. Let stand 5 minutes. Remove from cups. Slice and serve warm or cool completely on wire rack, wrap tightly and store overnight.

Yield:   6 loaves

See page 44 for conventional directions.

# busy-day meatloaf

1 cup Croutettes herb seasoned croutons
1/2 cup milk
1 egg
2 teaspoons Worcestershire sauce
1/4 cup finely chopped onion
1 teaspoon salt
1 lb. ground beef
Catsup or chili sauce

- Combine Croutettes croutons and milk in large mixing bowl. Let stand about 5 minutes or until croutons are softened. Add egg, Worcestershire sauce, onion and salt. Beat well. Add ground beef. Mix until combined.

- Press meat mixture evenly in ungreased 9 x 5 x 3-inch glass loaf pan. Score loaf by making several diagonal grooves across top. Fill with cat-sup.

- Microwave on full power 6 minutes. Rotate and microwave on full power 5 minutes longer. Cover and let stand 5 minutes before serving.

Yield:   6 servings

See page 95 for conventional directions.

# corn-crisped chicken

**1/3 cup Corn Flake Crumbs**
**1/4 teaspoon salt**
**1/8 teaspoon pepper**
**1/4 cup evaporated milk**
   **1 whole chicken breast, split, washed and patted dry**

- Combine Corn Flake Crumbs, salt and pepper in shallow dish.

- Dip chicken in milk. Coat with Crumbs mixture. Place in shallow glass baking dish. Cover with waxed paper or plastic wrap. Poke several holes in plastic wrap to allow steam to escape.

- Microwave on full power about 8 minutes or until chicken is tender.

Yield:   2 servings

See page 124 for conventional directions.

# Mexican stuffed peppers

**6 large green peppers**
**Salt**
**1 lb. ground beef**
**1 medium-size onion, sliced**
**2-1/2 cups Rice Krispies cereal**
**1/8 teaspoon instant minced garlic**
**2 teaspoons chili powder**
**1 teaspoon salt**
**1/8 teaspoon pepper**
**1 teaspoon sugar**
**1/2 cup sliced, pitted, ripe olives**
**1 can (6 oz.) tomato paste**
**1 can (16 oz.) whole peeled tomatoes, drained**
**1/2 cup shredded sharp cheddar cheese**

- Wash peppers. Cut off tops and remove seedy portions. Lightly salt inside of each pepper. Place peppers, cut side up, in 12 x 7-1/2 x 2-inch glass baking dish. Set aside.

- Place ground beef and onion in 8 x 8 x 2-inch glass baking dish. Stir to crumble. Microwave on full power 6 to 7 minutes or until beef is cooked, stirring occasionally. Drain off excess drippings. Add remaining ingredients except cheese. Stir to combine, cutting tomatoes into pieces with spoon. Spoon into peppers, dividing evenly. Cover stuffed peppers with plastic wrap. Poke several holes in plastic wrap to allow steam to escape.

- Microwave on full power about 15 minutes or until filling is thoroughly heated and peppers are tender. Sprinkle tops with cheese. Microwave on full power until cheese melts.

Yield:   6 servings

See page 91 for conventional directions.

**1 cup Corn Flake Crumbs**

**1 teaspoon salt**

**1/4 teaspoon pepper**

**1 tablespoon prepared mustard**

**1/3 cup milk**

**1 lb. ground beef**

**1 egg**

**2 cups seasoned, stiff mashed potatoes**

**1/4 cup chopped onion**

**2 teaspoons dried parsley flakes**

**1/2 cup shredded American cheese**

**2 tablespoons regular margarine or butter, melted**

**Paprika**

- Measure 1/2 cup of the Corn Flake Crumbs, the salt, pepper, mustard and milk into large mixing bowl. Beat well. Add ground beef. Mix until combined. Spread evenly around sides and in bottom of ungreased 9-inch glass pie plate to form meat pie shell. Set aside.

- In small mixing bowl, beat egg slightly. Add potatoes, onion, parsley flakes and cheese. Stir until combined. Spread potato mixture evenly over meat mixture.

- Microwave on full power 15 to 18 minutes or until meat is completely cooked. While pie is baking, combine the remaining 1/2 cup Corn Flake Crumbs with melted margarine. Set aside.

- Remove pie from oven. Sprinkle Crumbs mixture evenly over top. Microwave on full power 1 minute longer. Sprinkle with paprika.

Yield:   6 servings

See page 98 for conventional directions.

# pineapple ham loaf

2 cups 40% Bran Flakes cereal

1/2 cup milk

1 egg

1 lb. ground cooked ham

1 lb. ground uncooked pork

1/4 cup finely chopped onion

2 tablespoons finely chopped green pepper

1/2 teaspoon salt

1/4 teaspoon pepper

2 teaspoons prepared mustard

1/4 cup firmly packed brown sugar

1 can (8 oz.) sliced pineapple, drained, reserving syrup for Sweet and Sour Sauce

- In large mixing bowl, combine 40% Bran Flakes cereal and milk. Let stand 1 to 2 minutes or until cereal is softened.

- Add egg. Mix well. Add ham, pork, onion, green pepper, salt, pepper and mustard. Mix until combined. Gently press evenly in ungreased 8 x 8 x 2-inch glass baking dish. Sprinkle sugar over top of meat mixture. Arrange pineapple slices over sugar.

- Microwave on full power about 25 minutes or until meat thermometer inserted in center reaches 170° F. Cover and let stand 10 minutes before serving. Serve with *Sweet and Sour Sauce*.

Yield:   8 to 10 servings

# sweet and sour sauce

Water

Reserved pineapple syrup from Pineapple Ham Loaf

5 teaspoons cornstarch

1/3 cup firmly packed brown sugar

3 tablespoons vinegar

1 teaspoon prepared mustard

188

- Add water to reserved pineapple syrup to measure 1-1/4 cups. Set aside.

- In 4-cup glass measuring cup, mix together cornstarch and sugar. Stir in syrup mixture, vinegar and mustard. Cover with waxed paper or plastic wrap. Poke several holes in plastic wrap to allow steam to escape.

- Microwave on full power until mixture boils. Microwave on full power about 2 minutes longer or until sauce is thickened and clear.

Yield:   1-1/3 cups

# festive corn custard

3 eggs, slightly beaten
1-1/2 cups milk
1/2 teaspoon salt
1 teaspoon sugar
1/4 cup finely chopped onion
2 cups Croutettes herb seasoned croutons
1 can (12 oz.) whole kernel corn with sweet peppers, drained
1/4 cup sliced, pitted, ripe olives

- Combine all ingredients in large mixing bowl. Portion evenly into six 6-ounce glass custard cups. Place in shallow glass baking dish filled with about 1 inch of hot water.

- Microwave on full power 8 minutes. Rotate and microwave on full power about 9 minutes longer or until knife inserted near center comes out clean. Let stand 5 minutes before serving.

NOTE:  Custards may cook at slightly different rates because amount of custard in each cup tends to vary.

Yield:   6 servings

See page 75 for conventional directions.

# stuffing squares

**1 egg**
**1 can (10-3/4 oz.) condensed cream of mushroom soup**
**1 cup water**
**1 package (7 oz., 7 cups) Croutettes herb seasoned croutons**

- In large mixing bowl, beat egg until foamy. Add soup and water, stirring until well combined.

- Add Croutettes croutons all at one time, tossing lightly until croutons are evenly and thoroughly moistened. Spoon into ungreased 8 x 8 x 2-inch glass baking dish, pressing lightly.

- Microwave on full power about 6 minutes or until set. Cut into squares to serve.

Yield:   9 servings

See page 76 for conventional directions and variations.

# crunchy Rice Krispies topping

**1 tablespoon regular margarine or butter**
**1 cup Rice Krispies cereal**

- Microwave margarine in 8 x 8 x 2-inch glass baking dish on full power until melted. Add Rice Krispies cereal, stirring until well coated. Microwave on full power 1-1/2 to 2 minutes or until cereal is crisp. Sprinkle over hot soup, crisp green salad or casserole just before serving.

Yield:   1 cup

See page 78 for conventional directions and variations.

# carrots au gratin

**5 tablespoons regular margarine or butter**

**1/2 cup Corn Flake Crumbs**

**1/3 cup chopped onion**

**3 tablespoons regular all-purpose flour**

**1 teaspoon salt**

**1/8 teaspoon pepper**

**1-1/2 cups milk**

**1 cup shredded American cheese**

**4 cups sliced carrots, cooked and drained (about 1-1/2 lbs.)**

**1 tablespoon dried parsley flakes**

● In small glass mixing bowl, microwave 2 tablespoons of the margarine on full power until melted. Combine with Corn Flake Crumbs. Set aside for topping.

● Measure the remaining 3 tablespoons margarine and the onion into 4-cup glass measuring cup. Microwave on full power 1-1/2 to 2 minutes or until onion is tender. Stir in flour, salt and pepper. Add milk gradually, stirring until smooth. Microwave on full power 5 to 6 minutes or until bubbly and thickened, stirring twice during cooking time. Add cheese, stirring until melted. Pour into ungreased 12 x 7-1/2 x 2-inch glass baking dish. Stir in carrots and parsley flakes.

● Microwave on full power 8 to 10 minutes or until thoroughly heated and bubbly.

● Sprinkle Crumbs mixture evenly over top. Microwave on full power 1 minute longer. Let stand 5 minutes before serving.

Yield:   8 servings

See page 80 for conventional directions.

# herbed zucchini bake

**6 cups cubed zucchini squash (about 3 medium-size)**
**3/4 cup grated carrots**
**1/2 cup chopped onions**
**1-1/2 cups Croutettes herb seasoned croutons**
**1 can (10-3/4 oz.) condensed cream of chicken soup**
**1/2 cup dairy sour cream**
**1 tablespoon chopped pimiento**
**1 teaspoon salt**
**1/4 teaspoon pepper**

- Stir together zucchini squash, carrots and onions in 10 x 6 x 2-inch glass baking dish. Cover with waxed paper or plastic wrap. Poke several holes in plastic wrap to allow steam to escape. Microwave on full power about 7 minutes or until tender. Drain vegetables. Set vegetables and baking dish aside.

- In medium-size mixing bowl, stir together Croutettes croutons, soup, sour cream, pimiento, salt and pepper. Mix thoroughly. Stir in squash, carrots and onions. Mix well. Spread mixture evenly in the 10 x 6 x 2-inch glass baking dish.

- Microwave on full power about 8 minutes or until thoroughly heated and bubbly. Cover and let stand 5 minutes before serving.

Yield:   8 servings

See page 81 for conventional directions.

# Danish dessert

**1 package (4-3/4 oz.) Junket Danish Dessert, any flavor**
**2 cups cold water**

- In 4-cup glass measuring cup, stir Danish Dessert into water. Cover with waxed paper or plastic wrap. Poke several holes in plastic wrap to allow steam to escape.

- Microwave on full power about 6 minutes or until thickened and clear, stirring every 2 minutes. Pour into dessert dishes. Chill 3 to 4 hours.

Yield:   4 servings

# peanut butter clusters

**1 package (6 oz., 1 cup) butterscotch morsels**
**1/4 cup peanut butter**
**3 cups Product 19 multivitamin and iron supplement cereal**

- Microwave butterscotch morsels and peanut butter together in 4-cup glass measuring cup on full power for 2 minutes. Stir until smooth. Add Product 19 supplement cereal. Stir until well coated.

- Drop by level measuring-tablespoon onto buttered baking sheet. Chill until firm.

Yield:   about 2 dozen

See page 178 for conventional directions.

# date 'n honey pie

**1/4 cup regular margarine or butter, softened**
**1/3 cup honey**
**2/3 cup corn syrup**
**3 eggs**
**1 teaspoon vanilla flavoring**
**3/4 cup All-Bran cereal or Bran Buds cereal**
**3/4 cup cut, pitted dates**
**1 baked 9-inch pie crust in glass pie plate**

- In large mixing bowl, beat margarine, honey and corn syrup until well blended. Add eggs. Beat until smooth. Stir in vanilla, All-Bran cereal and dates. Pour into baked pie crust.

- Microwave on full power 4 minutes. Rotate and microwave on full power 6 to 8 minutes longer or until knife inserted near center comes out clean. Cool completely before cutting. Top each serving with ice cream or whipped topping, if desired.

Yield:   one 9-inch pie

See page 146 for conventional directions.

# all-American party pudding

1/3 cup seedless raisins
20 Frosted Mini-Wheats biscuits or Toasted Mini-Wheats biscuits
3 eggs
1/2 cup granulated sugar or firmly packed brown sugar
1/2 teaspoon salt
1 teaspoon vanilla flavoring
2 tablespoons regular margarine or butter
2 cups milk

- Sprinkle raisins evenly in ungreased 10 x 6 x 2-inch glass baking dish. Place Frosted Mini-Wheats biscuits, frosted side up, in single layer over raisins. Set aside.

- In medium-size mixing bowl, beat eggs until foamy. Add sugar, salt, vanilla and margarine, mixing only until combined. In 2-cup glass measuring cup, microwave milk on full power about 2 minutes or until scalded. Gradually add hot milk to egg mixture, stirring constantly until margarine is melted. Pour milk mixture evenly over biscuits.

- Microwave on full power 4 minutes. Rotate and microwave on full power 4 minutes and 15 seconds longer. Cover and let stand 5 minutes. Cut into squares. Serve warm with half-and-half or ice cream.

Yield:   6 servings

See page 135 for conventional directions.


# magic cookie bars

1/3 cup regular margarine or butter
1-1/2 cups Corn Flake Crumbs
3 tablespoons sugar
1 cup coarsely chopped walnuts
1 package (6 oz., 1 cup) semi-sweet chocolate morsels
1 can (3-1/2 oz., 1-1/3 cups) flaked coconut
1 can (15 oz.) sweetened condensed milk

- Microwave margarine in 12 x 7-1/2 x 2-inch glass baking dish on full power until melted. Add Corn Flake Crumbs and sugar. Mix thoroughly. Press lightly in bottom of dish to form crust.

- Sprinkle walnuts, chocolate morsels and coconut evenly over Crumbs crust. Pour sweetened condensed milk evenly over top.

- Microwave on full power about 7 minutes or until lightly browned around edges. Cool completely before cutting into bars.

Yield:   42 bars, 1 x 2 inches

See page 170 for conventional directions.

# easy Pop-Tarts crumble

**4 brown sugar-cinnamon Frosted Pop-Tarts pastries**

**3 tablespoons regular margarine or butter**

**1 can (1 lb. 5 oz.) apple or blueberry pie filling**

**1 tablespoon lemon juice**

**1/2 teaspoon ground cinnamon**

- Crumble Pop-Tarts pastries into small pieces. Place in medium-size mixing bowl. Set aside.

- Microwave margarine on full power until melted. Pour over crumbled pastries, tossing with fork until well combined. Set aside.

- In 8 x 8 x 2-inch glass baking dish, stir together pie filling, lemon juice and cinnamon. Sprinkle crumbled pastries mixture evenly over top.

- Microwave on full power about 6 minutes or until bubbly. Serve warm with whipped topping or ice cream, if desired.

Yield:   6 servings

See page 141 for conventional directions and variations.

# bran custard surprise

        2 eggs
1-1/3 cups milk
    1/8 teaspoon salt
    1/8 teaspoon ground nutmeg
    1/3 cup sugar
    1/2 teaspoon vanilla flavoring
    2/3 cup Cracklin' Bran cereal
    1/4 cup seedless raisins

- In medium-size mixing bowl, beat eggs until foamy. Stir in remaining in-gredients. Portion evenly into four 6-ounce glass custard cups. Place in shallow glass baking dish filled with about 1 inch of hot water.

- Microwave on full power 6 minutes. Rotate and microwave on full power about 6 minutes longer or until knife inserted near center comes out clean. Let stand 5 minutes before serving. Serve warm with ice cream or whipped topping, if desired.

Yield:   4 servings

NOTE:   Custards may cook at slightly different rates because amount of custard in each cup tends to vary.

See page 149 for conventional directions.

# raisin bran toffee squares

    1 cup regular all-purpose flour
1/2 teaspoon baking powder
1/2 teaspoon salt
    2 cups Raisin Bran cereal
3/4 cup milk
1/2 cup regular margarine or butter, softened
    1 cup firmly packed brown sugar
    2 eggs
    1 teaspoon vanilla flavoring

- Stir together flour, baking powder and salt. Set aside.

- In small mixing bowl, combine Raisin Bran cereal and milk. Let stand 1 to 2 minutes or until cereal is softened.

- In medium-size mixing bowl, beat margarine and sugar until light and fluffy. Add eggs and vanilla. Beat well. Stir in cereal mixture. Add flour mixture. Mix well. Spread batter evenly in ungreased 8 x 8 x 2-inch glass baking dish.

- Microwave on full power about 10 minutes or until wooden pick inserted near center comes out clean. Rotate every 3 minutes. Cool completely. Spread with *Confectioners' Sugar Frosting* (see page 168).

Yield:   16 squares, 2 x 2 inches

# easy-roll pie crust

**1/4 cup All-Bran cereal, Bran Buds cereal or Corn Flake Crumbs**
   **1 cup regular all-purpose flour**
**1/8 teaspoon salt**
**1/4 cup shortening**
   **5 tablespoons cold water**

- Stir together All-Bran cereal, flour and salt in medium-size mixing bowl. Cut in shortening until pieces are size of small peas. Sprinkle water over cereal mixture. Mix gently with fork until mixture holds together.

- On lightly floured surface, roll dough to a 10-inch circle. Place in ungreased 9-inch glass pie plate. Flute edges. Prick bottom and sides with fork.

- Microwave on full power 3 minutes. Rotate and microwave about 2 minutes longer or until center no longer appears doughy. Cool completely. Use for any refrigerated or frozen filling.

Yield:   one 9-inch pie crust

# marshmallow treats

1/4 cup regular margarine or butter
1 package (10 oz., about 40) regular marshmallows
    or 4 cups miniature marshmallows
5 cups Rice Krispies cereal

● Place margarine and marshmallows in 12 x 7-1/2 x 2-inch glass baking dish. Microwave on full power 2 minutes. Stir to combine. Microwave on full power 2 minutes longer. Stir until smooth.

● Add Rice Krispies cereal. Stir until well coated. Using buttered spatula or waxed paper, press mixture evenly in dish. Cut into squares when cool.

Yield: 15 squares

See page 159 for conventional directions and variations.


# crunchy party snack

4 cups Croutettes herb seasoned croutons
1 cup salted cocktail peanuts
1 cup thin pretzel sticks
1/2 cup regular margarine or butter
2 tablespoons Worcestershire sauce

● Measure Croutettes croutons, peanuts and pretzels into 12 x 7-1/2 x 2-inch glass baking dish. Set aside.

● In glass measuring cup, microwave margarine on full power until melted. Stir in Worcestershire sauce. Pour over croutons mixture, tossing gently until well coated.

● Microwave on full power 3 minutes. Stir and microwave on full power 3 minutes longer. Cool completely. Store in tightly covered container.

Yield: 5-1/2 cups

See page 15 for conventional directions.

# French cherry dessert

1/2 cup regular margarine or butter, softened

   3 tablespoons sifted confectioners' sugar

1/2 cup regular all-purpose flour

1/2 cup Corn Flake Crumbs

        *        *        *        *        *

1/4 cup regular all-purpose flour

1/2 teaspoon baking powder

1/4 teaspoon salt

   2 eggs

   1 cup granulated sugar

   1 teaspoon vanilla flavoring

1/2 cup coarsely chopped nuts

1/2 cup flaked coconut

1/2 cup finely chopped maraschino cherries

     Whipped topping or vanilla ice cream

- In small mixing bowl, beat margarine and confectioners' sugar until smooth and creamy. Stir in the 1/2 cup flour and the Corn Flake Crumbs. Spread mixture evenly in bottom of ungreased 8 x 8 x 2-inch glass baking dish.

- Microwave on full power about 3 minutes or until crust springs back when lightly touched. Set aside.

- Stir together the 1/4 cup flour, the baking powder and salt. Set aside.

- In medium-size mixing bowl, beat eggs slightly. Stir in granulated sugar and vanilla. Add flour mixture, mixing until well combined. Reserve 2 tablespoons nuts and 2 tablespoons coconut for topping. Stir in remaining nuts, remaining coconut and the cherries. Spread mixture over crust.

- Microwave on full power 4 minutes. Sprinkle with the reserved nuts and coconut. Microwave on full power about 4 minutes longer or until mixture is set. Cool. Cut into squares and serve with whipped topping or a small scoop of vanilla ice cream.

Yield:  9 servings

See page 133 for conventional directions.

# crunchy bran jumble

**3 cups Cracklin' Bran cereal**
**1 cup salted cocktail peanuts**
**1 cup thin pretzel sticks**
**1/3 cup regular margarine or butter**
**1 tablespoon sesame seed**
**1/2 teaspoon ground oregano**
**1 teaspoon onion salt**
**2 teaspoons Worcestershire sauce**

- Measure Cracklin' Bran cereal, peanuts and pretzels into 12 x 7-1/2 x 2-inch glass baking dish. Set aside.

- In glass measuring cup, microwave margarine on full power until melted. Stir in remaining ingredients. Pour over cereal mixture, stirring until well coated.

- Microwave on full power 3 minutes. Stir carefully and microwave on full power 3 minutes longer. Cool completely. Store in tightly covered container.

Yield:   5 cups

See page 15 for conventional directions.

200

# product index

# general index